INSIGHTS INTO WOMENPOWER DEVELOPMENT

Insights into Womenpower Development

By
Trilok Singh

CYBER TECH PUBLICATIONS
4264/3, Ansari Road, Daryaganj, New Delhi-110002 (India)
Ph.: 011-23244078. Fax: 011-23280028
E-Mail: cyberpublicationsdelhi@yahoo.com

Insights into Womenpower Development

Trilok Singh

First Edition 2011

Published by G.S. Rawat
For Cyber Tech Publications
4264/3, Ansari Road, Daryaganj, New Delhi-110002
Ph.: 011-23244078, 43559448 Fax: 011-23280028
E-Mail: cyberpublicationsdelhi@yahoo.com
E-mail: cybertechpublications@gmail.com
Website: www.cybertechpublications.com

Printed at
Asian offset printers.

Contents

Preface

> "Be unselfish. That is the first and final commandment for those who would be useful, and happy in their usefulness. If you think of yourself only, you cannot develop because you are choking the source of development, which is spiritual expansion through thought for others."
>
> —*Dr. Charles W. Eliot*

In demographic sense women constitute half of the world population with varying spatial distribution. But discrimination on one count or another against women is prevalent everywhere with varying degree of magnitude. Womenpower is not recognized and utilized in proper way. Hence the need of womenpower development, which is a prerequisite of alround progress.

The present book intends to recognize the potential of womenpower in social, political and economic terms. Judiciously selected valuable information is collated herein under the following chapters—Womenpower: An Observation; Development Process and Women; Strategies; Women's Reservations Bill; Indian Scenario and Statutory Measures; Womenpower After Constitution (73rd) Amendment; Womenpower and Rural Development; Womenpower—The Neglected Factor in Development; Women Under Globalisation & Bibliography.

Obviously this will delight and enlighten researchers, teachers, social scientists, policy planners and social and women activists besides NGOs and voluntary organizations operating in the field.

In course of furnishing authentic information, we have consulted a number of sources—both primary and secondary, and subscribed them by way of citation or substantial reproduction. I am deeply beholden to all the experts in the field whose views/works are made use of in this work. I am equally grateful to their publishers and copyright holders. Efforts are made to acknowledge them in references and bibliography.

Simultaneously I was much benefited by inspiration, guidance and assistance of my seniors, colleagues and friends. Besides these librarieans and other staff at different libraries has extended their cooperation by making available the requisite reading materials at their helms. I am thankful to them also.

Finally, I express my gratitude to my publishers for evincing keen interests in this project and also bringing out this on shortest possible time.

Comments and criticism from learned readers are welcome which we will incorporate in subsequent edition with due acknowledgement.

—Author

1

Womenpower: An Observation

> "For what reason, then, should the woman worker seek a union with the bourgeois feminists? Who, in actual fact, would stand to gain in the event of such an alliance? Certainly not the woman worker."
>
> —***Alexandra Kollontai, 1909***

As our intention here is to depict different aspects of emancipation of womenpower, we must understand first fundamental theories, concepts and practices of empowerment.

In fact the phrase Human Empowerment covers a vast rare landscape of meanings, interpretations, definitions and disciplines ranging from psychology and philosophy to the highly commercialized Self-Help industry and Motivational sciences. Sociological empowerment often addresses members of groups that social discrimination processes have excluded from decision-making processes through - for example - discrimination based on disability, race, ethnicity, religion, or gender.

Empowerment as a methodology is often associated with feminism and consciousness-raising.

Marginalisation

By "Marginalized" we mean to the overt or covert trends within societies whereby those perceived as lacking desirable traits or deviating from the group norms tend to be excluded by wider society and ostracised as undesirables. Sometimes groups are marginalized by society at large, but governments are often unwitting or enthusiastic participants.

For example, the U.S. government marginalized cultural minorities, particularly blacks, prior to the Civil Rights Act of 1964. This Act made it illegal to restrict access to schools and public places based on race. Equal opportunity laws which actively oppose such marginalization, allow increased empowerment to occur. It should be noted that they are also a symptom of minorities' and women's empowerment through lobbying. Marginalized people who have no opportunities for self-sufficiency become, at a minimum, dependent on charity or welfare. They lose their self-confidence because they cannot be fully self-supporting. The opportunities denied them also deprive them of the pride of accomplishment which others, who have those opportunities, can develop for themselves.

This in turn can lead to psychological, social and even mental health problems. Empowerment is then the process of obtaining these basic opportunities for marginalized people, either directly by those people, or through the help of non-marginalized others who share their own access to these opportunities. It also includes actively thwarting attempts to deny those opportunities.

Empowerment also includes encouraging, and developing the skills for, self-sufficiency, with a focus on eliminating the future need for charity or welfare in the individuals of the group. This process can be difficult to start and to implement effectively, but there are many examples of empowerment projects with success.

Coming to strategies, one empowerment strategy is to assist marginalized people to create their own nonprofit organization, using the rationale that only the marginalized people, themselves, can know what their own people need most, and that control of the organization by outsiders can actually help to further entrench marginalization.

Charitable organizations lead from outside of the community, for example, can disempower the community by entrenching a dependence on charity or welfare. A nonprofit organization can target strategies that cause structural changes, reducing the need for ongoing dependence. Red Cross, for example, can focus on improving the health of indigenous people, but does not have authority in its charter to install water-delivery and purification systems, even though the lack of such a system profoundly, directly and negatively impacts health.

A nonprofit composed of the indigenous people, however, could insure their own organization does have such authority and could set their own agendas, make their own plans, seek the needed resources, do as much of the work as they can, and take responsibility - and credit - for the success of their projects (or the consequences, should they fail). Varions critical perspectives exist that propose that an empowerment paradigm is present, Clark (2008) showed that whilst there was a degree of autonomy provided by empowerment, it also made way for extended surveillance and control, hence the contradiction perspective (Fardini, 2001).

Process of Empowerment

In simple words, empowerment is the process which

enables one to gain power, authority and influence over others, institutions or society. Empowerment is the process that allows one to gain the knowledge, skill-sets and attitude needed to cope with the changing world and the circumstances in which one lives. Empowerment in the workplace is regarded by critics as more a pseudo-empowerment exercise, the idea of which is to change the attitudes of workers, so as to make them work harder rather than giving them any real power, and Wilkinson (1998) refers to this as "attitudinal shaping".

What is Empowerment?

(1) Having decision-making power of one's own

(2) Having access to information and resources for taking proper decision

(3) Having a range of options from which you can make choices (not just yes/no, either/or.)

(4) Ability to exercise assertiveness in collective decision making

(5) Having positive thinking on the ability to make change

(6) Ability to learn skills for improving one's personal or group power.

(7) Ability to change others' perceptions by democratic means.

(8) Involving in the growth process and changes that is never ending and self-initiated

(9) Increasing one's positive self-image and overcoming stigma

(10) Increasing one's ability in discreet thinking to sort out right and wrong

Recent research suggests that the opportunity to exercise personal discretion/choice (and complete meaningful work) is an important element contributing to employee engagement and well-being. There is evidence that initiative and motivation are increased when people have a more positive attributional style. This influences self-belief, resilience when faced with setbacks, and the ability to visualize oneself overcoming problems. The implication is that 'empowerment' suits some more than others, and should be positioned in the broader and wider context of an 'enabling' work environment. Empowerment to employees in the work place provides them with opportunities to make their own decisions with regards to their tasks.

Nowadays more and more bosses and managers are practicing the concept of empowerment among their subordinates to provide them with better opportunities. In economic development, the empowerment approach focuses on mobilizing the self-help efforts of the poor, rather than providing them with social welfare. Economic empowerment is also the empowering of previously disadvantaged sections of the population, for example, in many previously colonized African and Asian nations..

Personal Development

It is pertinent to note that in the arena of personal development, empowerment forms an apogee of many a system of Self Realization or of identity (re-)formation. Realizing the solipsistic impracticality of everyone anarchistically attempting to exercise power over everyone else, empowerment advocates have adopted the word "empowerment" to offer the attractions of such power, but they generally constrain its individual exercise to potentiality and to feel-good uses within the individual psyche. The concept of personal development is seen as important by many employers, with emphasis placed on continuous learning, increased self-awareness and emotional intelligence.

Empowerment is ultimately driven by the individual's belief in their capability to influence events. Empowerment can be attained through one or many ways. An important factor in the discovery and application of the human "self empowerment" lies within the tools used to unveil the truth. It has been suggested that Yoga is one such tool that can be used for more than the obvious physical benefits. When Yoga is practiced consistently the mind / body connection is apparent.

Through this connection, the individual finds him or herself with a stronger sense of self and the ability to change areas where bad habits rule, negative emotions run rampant, even controlling addictions through understanding them for what they are. What can be more empowering than gaining control over self. Gender is an important area of study in many disciplines, such as literary theory, drama studies, film theory, performance theory, contemporary art history, anthropology, sociology, psychology and psychoanalysis. These disciplines sometimes differ in their approaches to how and why they study gender.

For instance in anthropology, sociology and psychology, gender is often studied as a practice, whereas in cultural studies representations of gender are more often examined.

Gender studies is also a discipline in itself: an interdisciplinary area of study that incorporates methods and approaches from a wide range of disciplines. Some feminist critics have dismissed the work of Sigmund Freud as sexist, because of his view that women are 'mutilated and must learn to accept their lack of a penis' (in Freud's terms a "deformity"). On the other hand, feminist theorists such as Juliet Mitchell, Nancy Chodorow, Jessica Benjamin, Jane Gallop, Bracha Ettinger, Shoshana Felman, Griselda

Pollock and Jane Flax have argued that psychoanalytic theory is vital to the feminist project and must, like other theoretical traditions, be adapted by women to free it from vestiges of sexism.

Shulamith Firestone, in "Freudianism: The Misguided Feminism", discusses how Freudianism is *almost* completely accurate, with the exception of one crucial detail: everywhere that Freud writes "penis", the word should be replaced with "power". Lacan's theory of sexuation organizes femininity and masculinity according to different unconscious structures. Both male and female subjects participate in the "phallic" organization, and the feminine side of sexuation is "supplementary" and not opposite or complementary. Sexuation (sexual situation) — the development of gender-roles and role-play in childhood — breaks down concepts of gender identity as innate or biologically determined.

Critics like Elizabeth Grosz accuse Jacques Lacan of maintaining a sexist tradition in psychoanalysis. Others, such as Judith Butler, Bracha Ettinger and Jane Gallop have used Lacanian work, though in a critical way, to develop gender theory. Julia Kristeva has significantly developed the field of semiotics. In her work on abjection, she structures subjectivity upon the abjection of the mother and argues that the way in which an individual excludes (or abjects) their mother as means of forming an identity is similar to the way in which societies are constructed. She contends that patriarchal cultures, like individuals, have had to exclude the maternal and the feminine so that they can come into being.

Notably, Mark Blechner expanded psychoanalytic views of sex and gender, calling psychoanalysis "the once and future queer science." He has argued that there is a "gender fetish" in western society, in which the gender of sexual partners is given enormously disproportionate attention over other factors involved in sexual attraction, such as age and social class. He proposes that the words "homosexuality" and "heterosexuality" be given prefixes, depending on the dimension that is the same or different between partners. "Age heterosexuality" would indicate an attraction between people of different ages, for example. What is conventionally called "heterosexuality" (attraction between a man and a woman) would be called "gender heterosexuality."

Cultures can have very different norms of maleness and masculinity. Blechner identifies the terror, in Western males, of penetration. Yet in many societies, being gay is defined only by being a male who lets himself be penetrated. Males who penetrate other males are considered masculine and not gay and are not the targets of prejudice.

In other cultures, however, receptive fellatio is the norm for early adolescence and seen as a requirement for developing normal manliness. The emergence of post-feminism affected gender studies, causing a movement in theories identity away from the concept of fixed or essentialist gender identity, to post-modern fluid or multiple identities.

It is remarkable that women's studies is an interdisciplinary academic field devoted to topics concerning women, feminism, gender, and politics. It often includes feminist theory, women's history (e.g. a history of women's suffrage) and social history, women's fiction, women's health, feminist psychoanalysis and the feminist and gender studies-influenced practice of most of the humanities and social sciences. The concept of gender performativity is at the core of Butler's work, notably in *Gender Trouble*. In Butler's terms the performance of gender, sex, and sexuality is about power in society. She locates the construction of the "gendered, sexed, desiring subject" in "regulative discourses."

A part of Butler's argument concerns the role of sex in the construction of "natural" or coherent gender and sexuality. In her account, gender and heterosexuality are constructed as natural because the opposition of the male and female sexes is constructed as natural. Women's Rights—legal, political, and social rights for women equal to those of men. Among these rights are control of property, equality of opportunity in education and employment, suffrage, and sexual freedom.

The women's rights movement, also known as feminism and women's liberation, arose in Europe in the late 18th century. Although today most women throughout the world have gained many rights according to law, in fact complete political, economic, and social equality with men remains to be achieved. In early societies, women bore and raised children, cared for the home, and helped maintain the family's economic production.

Men hunted, waged war, and, in settled agrarian societies, assumed primary responsibility for field crop production. Because of women's varied domestic activities, it is likely that they were responsible for the invention of weaving and potting.

Some scholars argue that the discovery throughout the European continent and the Near East of thousands of stone figures of female goddesses dating from the Paleolithic period and later indicates that these were originally goddess-worshipping, matricentric civilizations. Remarkably, male dominance, however, was preeminent from the time of the earliest written historical records, probably as a result of men's discovery of their role in conception as well as the development of hunting and warfare as prestige activities. The belief that women were naturally weaker and inferior to men also was sanctioned by god-centered religions.

In the Bible, God placed Eve under Adam's authority, and St. Paul urged Christian wives to be obedient to their husbands. In Hinduism the reward of a virtuous woman is rebirth as a man. Therefore, in most traditional societies, women generally were at a disadvantage. Their education was limited to learning domestic skills, and they had no access to positions of power.

Marriage was almost a necessity as a means of support or protection. Pressure was constant to produce many children. A married woman usually took her husband's status and lived with his family, with little recourse in case of ill treatment or nonsupport. Under Roman law, which influenced later European and American law, husband and wife were one, with the woman the possession of the man. As such, a woman had no legal control over her person, her own land and money, or her children.

It is noteworthy that as per a double standard of morality, respectable women had to be chaste but men did not. In the Middle Ages, feudal law, in which landholding carried with it military obligations, encouraged the subordination of women to men. Some exceptions to women's dependence on men did exist. In ancient Babylonia and Egypt women had property rights, and in medieval Europe they were permitted to join craft guilds. Some women had religious authority, for example, as Siberian shamans and Roman priestesses.

Occasionally women had political authority, such as Egyptian and Byzantine queens, heads of medieval nunneries, and Iroquois Indian women, who appointed men to clan and tribal councils. A few highly cultivated women flourished in ancient Rome, China, and in Renaissance Europe. During the French Revolution, women's republican clubs in France pleaded that the goals of liberty, equality, and fraternity should apply to all, regardless of sex. The subsequent adoption of the Code Napoleon, based on Roman law, however, obliterated any immediate realisation of such hopes on the Continent.

In England, Mary Wollstonecraft wrote *A Vindication of the Rights of Woman*(1792), the first major modern feminist work. Its demands for equality and its revolutionary tonε made it unacceptable at that time. Of deeper significance for women was the Industrial Revolution.

The transformation from handwork, which women had always carried on at home without pay, to machine-powered mass production meant that lower-class women could become wage earners in factories. This was the beginning of their independence, although factory conditions were hazardous and their pay, lower than men's, was legally controlled by their husbands.

At the same time middle- and upper-class women were expected to stay at home as idle, decorative symbols of their husbands' economic success. The only other option for respectable women of any class was work as governesses, clerks, shop assistants, and servants. Such conditions encouraged the feminist movement. On the Continent, feminist groups appeared sporadically but lacked strength. The Roman Catholic church opposed feminism on the grounds that it would destroy the patriarchal family. Agrarian countries held to traditional ideas, and in industrial countries feminist demands tended to be absorbed by the socialist movement. In largely Protestant, rapidly industrialising Great Britain and the U.S., feminism was more successful. The leaders were primarily educated, leisured, reform-minded women of the middle class. In 1848 more than 100 persons held the first women's rights convention, at Seneca Falls, N.Y. Led by the abolitionist Lucretia Mott and the feminist Elizabeth Cady Stanton, they demanded equal rights, including the right to vote, and an end to the double standard. British feminists first convened in 1855 behind the limited goal of property rights.

Remarkably, *The Subjection of Women* (1869) by the British philosopher John Stuart Mill focused public attention on their cause. Colleges were founded for women, such as Mount Holyoke (1837) in South Hadley, Mass, and Girton (1869) in Cambridge, England, although the right to admission to male-dominated universities took longer. Married women's property acts, passed in England in 1870 and at various times in the U.S., gave women control over their property.

Later, provisions were made for divorce, alimony, and child support. Labour legislation improved hours and wages for women. Suffrage, which came to be a primary goal of British and American feminists, encountered substantial resistance, despite massive and sometimes violent campaigns. In both countries the right to vote was only granted after World War I, partly in recognition of women's war contributions as paid and volunteer workers. After wars and revolutions in Russia (1917) and China (1949), new Communist governments discouraged the patriarchal family system and supported sexual equality, including birth control. In the Soviet Union, however, the majority of working women held low-paying jobs and were minimally represented in party and government councils.

Birth-control techniques were primitive, day-care centers were few, and working wives were responsible for keeping house and tending children. China more fully preserved its revolutionary ideals, but some job discrimination against women persisted. Socialist governments in Sweden in the 1930s established wide-ranging programs of equal rights for women, which included extensive child-care arrangements. In Britain and the U.S. progress was slower.

The number of working women increased substantially after the two World Wars, but they generally had low-paying, female-dominated occupations, such as schoolteaching and clerical work. Little opportunity existed in high-paying, male-dominated professions and major government posts. Advocates of birth control agitated for decades before women's right to family planning was recognised.

An Equal Rights Amendment (ERA) to the U.S. Constitution, to remove at one stroke legal, economic, and social restrictions on women, was introduced into Congress in 1923 but made no headway. Remarkably, in the 1960s, however, changing demographic, economic, and social patterns encouraged a resurgence of feminism. Lower infant mortality rates, soaring adult life expectancy, and the availability of the birth-control pill (after 1960) gave women greater freedom from child-care responsibilities.

These aspects, combined with inflation-which meant that many families needed two incomes-and a rising divorce rate, propelled more women into the job market. As working women encountered discrimination in many forms, the women's movement in the U.S. gained momentum. A presidential commission was established in 1960 to consider equal opportunities for women. Acts of Congress entitled them to equality in education, employment, and legal rights.

In 1964 the Civil Rights Act, initially intended only for blacks, was extended to women. In the late 1960s and early 1970s active feminists organised numerous women's rights groups. Notable among these is the National Organisation for Women founded by Betty Friedan and others in 1966 (which represented more than 250,000 members by the mid-1990s), and the National Abortion and Reproductive Rights Action League, founded three years later. In 1972 the Supreme Court declared that abortion was legal, and the ERA was passed by Congress and sent to the states for ratification.

By the June 1982 deadline, however, the ERA had been ratified by only 35 of the required 38 states. The women's movement questioned certain social institutions and traditional values, basing many of its arguments on scientific studies suggesting that most supposed differences between men and women result not from biology but from culture.

Many women objected that the English language itself by reflecting traditional male dominance in its word forms, perpetuated the problem. Successful efforts to reform the language included the introduction of the title *Ms.* as an alternative to *Miss* or *Mrs.;* the substitution of gender-neutral for gender-based terms, such as *firefighter* for *fireman* and *flight attedant* for *stewardess;* and the avoidance of the male pronoun *he*(for example, by the use of a phrase such as *he* or *she*) when referring to persons who may be either male or female.

The women's movement also sought to foster changes

in male-female relationships within the family, including the sharing of domestic roles and the avoidance of gender stereotyping in children's toys and books, television programs, and other media. An increasing number of women chose to use their maiden name after marriage, either in place of, or in conjunction with, their husband's name. Much attention was given to consciousness raising, to make women aware of their shared abilities, experiences, and problems.

While many feminist objectives enjoyed widespread support in the U.S., others were extremely controversial. The objectives included equal pay for equal work, federal support for day-care centers, recognition of lesbian rights, preservation of legal abortion and reproductive rights, and concerted action against rape, wife and child abuse, and discrimination against older and minority women. American women made many gains in the 1980s and '90s, while continuing to work to resolve the inequalities that still existed.

Women's groups campaigned effectively for the creation of rape hotlines and crisis centers, "date rape" prevention programs, and shelters for battered women. The political strides women have made in the U.S. may perhaps best be exemplified by the 1984 nomination of Geraldine Ferraro as the Democratic candidate for vice-president. Other women who have risen to positions of national prominence in recent decades include Supreme Court Justices Sandra Day O'Connor and Ruth Bader Ginsburg, Secretary of State Madeleine Albright, Attorney General Janet Reno (1938-).

It is pertinent to note that elsewhere in the world the women's rights movement has also made some progress. In nearly every nation, women have the right to vote and hold public office. Aided by the UN Commission on the

Status of Women (1946), women in many nations have gained legal rights and fuller access to education and the professions. However, the advent of industrialisation in non-Western nations has destroyed some traditional economic arrangements that favored women and has made underpaid factory labour the only work available to them, while the reappearance of fundamentalism (for example, in the Muslim world) has sometimes brought about the reemergence of oppressive practices.

In 1975, in recognition of International Women's Year, the UN launched the Decade for Women program. The UN Development Fund for Women (UNIFEM) was founded in 1976 as the Voluntary Fund for the UN Decade for Women, and it became a permanent organisation in autonomous association with the UN Development Program in 1985. In 1979 the UN General Assembly adopted a women's bill of rights, called the International Convention on the Elimination of All Forms of Discrimination Against Women (CEDAW).

Remarkably, educational reformers in the early 19th century became increasingly troubled by the chaotic absence of any system in American schools, particularly at the elementary, or common-school level. Leading educators such as Horace Mann in Massachusetts and Henry Barnard in Connecticut advocated systematic elementary education. The common-school reformers set forth optimistic arguments that education could transform all youth into literate, virtuous citizens, as well as nationalistic arguments that education could build a distinctive new society.

In addition, they appealed to people's fears about growing tensions and conflict in American society, stating that mass elementary schooling would preserve social stability and prevent crime and poverty. Repeatedly, the reformers contended that elementary education should be universally available and free, should be financed by public funds, and should be realised by public schools that were accountable to state governments.

It is pertinent to note here that by the end of 19th century they had achieved their goal: Universal, free public education was a reality. Beginning with Massachusetts (1852) and New York (1853), all states had passed compulsory school attendance laws by 1918. Not everyone, however, accepted public schools as the single best way to provide schooling. The most significant opposition came from American Roman Catholics, who believed that the moral values taught in public schools were biased toward Protestant beliefs. Arguing that sound education could not sever intellectual development from moral development, Roman Catholics created their own separate school system. Its position was strengthened in 1925 by the U.S. Supreme Court ruling that states could not compel children to attend public schools.

By 1990 about 14 per cent of American youth attended nonpublic schools. American higher education also expanded during the 19th century, but unlike elementary schooling, no public system developed that quickly overwhelmed private and religious institutions. Religious convictions motivated the creation of the earliest colleges, among them Harvard (1636), William and Mary (1693), and Yale (1701).

In the 19th century rivalry among Protestant denominations was one reason for the founding of hundreds of colleges. Despite their religious origins, many of these colleges were thought to serve nonreligious public purposes, and some received public assistance.

The lines between public and private remained blurred much longer in higher education than in elementary schooling. By the late 19th century, moreover, higher education seemed to confer benefits to society as a whole, and not only to those who attended college. Publicly supported state universities—especially those established or given federal assistance as a result of the land grants provided by the Morrill Act (1862), such as Kansas State University and the University of Wisconsin-were leaders in research that had practical application in fields such as agriculture, engineering, and public service. More basic research in the natural and social sciences flourished in private universities newly created to foster such study, for example, Johns Hopkins University (1876) and the University of Chicago (1890).

By 1900 higher education was a significant national resource; in that year, however, only 4 per cent of older American adolescents were enrolled in college. Mass higher education began in the 1950s and '60s. In 1990 more than 41 per cent of U.S. high school graduates enrolled in institutions of higher education. Education for younger adolescents—secondary education in the form of the high school and junior high (or middle) school—developed coherently and systematically only in the early 20th century, much later than the growth of elementary schools and colleges.

Before about 1900 a bewildering variety of institutions existed for the small percentage of teenagers who wanted to go beyond the common or elementary school, whether to learn a complex skill in lieu of increasingly unavailable on-the-job apprenticeships, or to prepare for college. Available institutions included private tutoring ventures, privately supported academies, and, beginning with Boston

English High School in 1821, public high schools. Nevertheless, it was only in 1874, in a Michigan Supreme Court decision involving the city of Kalamazoo, that it was clearly established that communities could use local property taxes to support high schools. In the hundred years that followed, the rise in high school attendance was one of the most striking features of American education. In 1880 only 2.5 per cent of American youth of high school age graduated from a secondary school; in 1990 about 75 per cent did so. More than any other educational institution, the public high school exemplified the American faith that schooling could successfully address a lengthening list of individual and social issues.

These concerns included preparation for college and for employment; preparation for many life activities; achieving social objectives such as the Americanisation of immigrants and the custodial care of youth who had no plans and nowhere else to go; and, at their most idealistic, meeting the societal objectives of social mobility and equality of opportunity.

Significantly, laws were passed that pushed compulsory attendance upward to the age of 14 in most states and to the age of 16 in many others. Beginning in 1794, with the establishment of the Board of Regents of the University of the State of New York, each state slowly created a department of education and enacted laws defining control and finance of public education within its borders. Although final authority resided with the state governments, the dominant American tradition has been one of decentralised administration.

The most significant unit of educational authority has been the local school district, the boundaries of which usually coincide with those of a city or town. Thus, American schools tend to reflect the educational values and financial capacities of the communities in which they are located. From earliest times, however, control of education by local communities was subjected to centralising pressures. Especially after the American Civil War, the states began to assert more aggressively the educational authority that technically they had always possessed.

State laws increasingly regulated compulsory school attendance, teacher qualifications, and sometimes curriculum content. In the 1970s state regulation was also applied to public school finance. Historically, local property taxes had been the principal means of raising revenues for both public elementary and secondary schools; dependence on this tax, however, meant that the wealth of the communities in which children lived determined the quality and extent of the schooling available to them. In the early 20th century, in order to help poorer communities, many states began to supplement local tax revenues with state funds. In the 1950s and '60s, when state programs to aid public higher education were expanded dramatically, general state revenues also largely financed such programs.

In 1971 a landmark decision by the California Supreme Court, *Serrano* v. *Priest*, determined that reliance on local property taxes to finance public schooling violated the California state constitution. Equalisation of educational expenditures among the school districts of a given state became a major educational issue. The possibility arose that in years to come public schooling in many states might be completely funded through state governments.

Further it is remarkable that weakening local autonomy was the modern social movement to increase the size, efficiency, and orderliness of public school systems and their administrative structures. For example, the position of the school superintendent increased in importance. The first public school superintendent was appointed in 1837, for Buffalo, N.Y.; by 1900 the superintendent was commonly regarded as the most influential figure in elementary and secondary education. In addition, school districts were consolidated and, though larger, were more unified. In 1900 more man 100,000 school districts existed in the U.S. By 1960 the number had fallen to about 40,000, and by the mid-1980s it had been further reduced to fewer than 15,000. Other centralising trends further eroded local control.

By 1870, American cities and rural areas had firmly established the modem pattern of age-graded classes, sequential promotion, and formal graduation after a stipulated number of years of school attendance. Even though the U.S. supposedly had no national system of education, the pattern of schooling was remarkably similar among American communities. The rise of mass-market textbook publishing companies and of educational testing organisations encouraged uniformity more than diversity.

Another pressure toward uniform organisation and standards came in the 1960s and '70s, when the teachers' unions demonstrated the power of large-scale collective bargaining in negotiating teachers' salaries, working conditions, and nonsalary benefits.

Role of Education

The most dramatic characteristic of the American educational system is the large number of people who have participated in it. The ideal of universal elementary education was largely achieved by the end of the 19th century, and in 1990 Americans who were 25 years of age or older had completed a median 12.4 years of schooling (in 1910 the median was 8 years).

Higher education, historically reserved for a privileged minority in the U.S. and in other countries as well, underwent remarkable growth after World War II; U.S. college enrollments soared from 2.6 million in 1950 to 13.7 million in 1990. No statistic better expresses the increasing egalitarianism of U.S. society or its popular consensus on the value of education. Such impressive statistics are easily misleading, however, for expanding educational opportunities were not equally available to all groups of Americans. The cultural and linguistic heritage of immigrant groups was ignored in the schools' single-minded concern for Americanisation. For religious communities such as the Amish, state insistence on compulsory attendance and a secular curriculum ran counter to their own fundamental beliefs.

The educational resources of most poor people were narrowly determined by the economic limitations of their communities. In the mid-20th century blacks and women commanded national attention, demanding equality of educational opportunity, which, for the first time, became a dominant objective of national educational policy. In American schools during the 1950s racial segregation was still prevalent. In the South separate schools for black and white youth were sanctioned by state laws that had been upheld by the U.S. Supreme Court. In the North no such laws existed; nevertheless, racial segregation was the common outcome in local schools fed by segregated neighborhoods and located in districts whose boundaries were deliberately drawn to ensure racial separation. Although all-black schools were supposedly equal in quality to all-white schools, and although some all-black schools-such as Dunbar High School in Washington, D.C.-were far more distinguished than most white schools, the nearly nationwide result of official or unofficial segregation was inferior education for blacks. In 1950 adult nonwhite males had completed a median 6.4 years of schooling, compared with 9.3 years for adult white males. In 1954, in *Brown* v. *Board of Education* of Topeka, Kans., the Supreme Court unanimously ruled that deliberate racial segregation in public schools was unconstitutional, thus overturning a policy it had first legitimised in 1896. Despite vigorous objections from many southern states, by 1980 the federal courts had largely succeeded in eliminating the "separate but equal" system of southern public schools. Most black Americans, however, lived in northern cities and not in the South.

In cities where intentional segregation was proven to exist, the courts ordered the redrawing of school district lines and sometimes ordered the busing of children from one neighborhood to another to achieve a racial balance. The use of judicial power to achieve desegregation and equality of opportunity had limits, however. Many whites had moved out of central cities by the 1970s, and in general the courts refused to sanction "metropolitan" busing plans-those that required busing between city and suburb-as a tool for achieving racial integration.

In a 1974 ruling, the Supreme Court, in effect, barred busing across school-district lines. Mere access to a school-educational opportunity in the narrowest sense-was increasingly regarded by educators and political leaders as an inadequate solution to the problem of educational inequality.

Special programs and resources were believed essential to guarantee genuine equality of education to disadvantaged youth. Whereas federal interest in school reform was confined in the late 1950s to promoting excellence in traditional academic fields, that interest soon shifted decisively to achieving social equity. Title I of the influential Elementary and Secondary Education Act (1965), passed under President Lyndon B. Johnson, provided federal funds for supplementary programs targeted toward poor and black children. Most Title I (later called Chapter I) funds were spent on elementary-age children, according to a prevailing theory that educational disadvantages could best be eliminated at an early age, before their cumulative effect was impossible to reverse. The federal Head Start program, established in 1965, extended remedial help to preschoolers. The strategies of targeted programs and categorical federal assistance were applied to other disadvantaged groups. The Bilingual Education Act, part of the 1967 amendments to the Elementary and Secondary Education Act, authorised federal funds for school districts having substantial numbers of students with limited mastery of English. In 1983 about $140 million was allocated to school districts for bilingual education programs to meet the needs of Hispanic and Asian children.

The Education for All Handicapped Children Act (1975) was a catalyst for providing new opportunities for other children with special needs. Problems of violence and apathy in many inner-city high schools also led to calls for federal programs to meet the needs of disadvantaged adolescents. Educational discrimination against women, although different from racial discrimination, was equally pervasive in U.S. society. Girls and boys in the 19th century were legally afforded equal educational opportunity; most public elementary schools were coeducational by the time of the American Revolution, and most public high schools became so after the Civil War. Even at the elementary level, however, girls were subtly but firmly taught that a woman's place is in the home only, rather than also in secondary schools, universities, and the professions. The first college to admit women alongside men was Oberlin College, coeducational since its founding in 1833. During this era, members of the first generation of women educational reformers; including Catharine Beecher (1800-78), Emma Willard, and Mary Lyon, established women's academies that provided female students with secondary and sometimes college-level education and offered subjects, such as mathematics, science, and history, that previously were considered unnecessary for women. The first successful women's college, Vassar College, opened in 1865. Not until the 20th century, however, did women in large numbers participate in higher education; even then, social expectations as well as male discrimination often closed career doors to well-educated women. Only in the 1960s did many of these barriers begin to recede.

Title IX of the federal Education Amendments of 1972 prohibited discrimination on the basis of sex in educational institutions that received federal aid.

It is significant to note that the most recent expression of the American tendency toward more schooling for more people was the extension of schooling opportunities to people both younger and older than the ages traditionally served by formal education. At the preprimary level, more children attended various kinds of nursery schools and day-care centers. In 1966 less than 30 per cent of American children age 3 to 5 were enrolled in preprimary programs; by 1990 almost 60 per cent participated in such programs.

If emphasis continues on programs for early education to compensate for educational disadvantages, and if more parents work, either in dual-career or single-parent households, the percentage of children in preprimary programs will probably continue to rise. Adult education, or "lifelong-learning" programs-usually defined as part-time study not directed toward a degree-also increased substantially. More than 23 million adults took part in such programs in 1984. Most of those enrolling in such programs do so for job-related reasons, although personal interests and hobbies are also significant motivations.

In general, people who have had previous experience with higher education are more likely to enroll in adult education classes than those who have not. With the recent decline in the adolescent population-those available for conventional college enrollment in the 1980s-many colleges, faced with excess capacity, vigorously promoted adult education as a means to boost enrollments.

This trend, together with a growing public realisation that human development continues beyond adolescence, will probably guarantee the continued expansion of this new sector of the educational market. Although people frequently behave as though education takes place only in schools and colleges, it in fact occurs in many settings, directly and indirectly, intentionally and unintentionally. Many educators in the 1970s and the '80s worked to improve the quality of education in nonschool settings. The instructional programs of museums, for example, were revised, and in cities such as Boston and San Francisco, museums were founded that were particularly oriented toward children.

Families gained access to an outpouring of books, courses, and workshops designed to teach parenting as a distinct skill. In the form of on-the-job training or staff development, education in the workplace also expanded.

Finally, highly professional organisations began to emerge in children's television in the 1960s, particularly the Children's Television Workshop, producing such shows as "Sesame Street" and "The Electric Company."

Role of Computer Education

It can be obvious the objectives assigned to formal education increased dramatically in the past century, the science and art of U.S. educational practice underwent no comparable revolution. Despite occasional experiments such as team teaching and ungraded primary classrooms, the essentials of American school practice in 1900 were all intact near the end of the 20th century: instruction in age-graded groups, in time periods of 30-60 minutes, with one adult teacher, leading to promotion or graduation primarily as a function of age. The influence of distinguished educators such as the American John Dewey has combined with the popularisation of psychoanalytic ideas to make American education substantially more child centered than it used to be. In addition, the gradual accumulation of knowledge about the different ways in which children learn and about the special needs of many children have led the elementary education system to be more sensitive to identifying and attending to individual differences.

Most so-called technological breakthroughs, such as the teaching-machine movement of the 1950s, proved to be mere fads and were short-lived. Whether the increasing availability of microcomputers or contemporary biomedical research (for example, on the human brain or in human genetics) will substantially alter educational practice is not yet known.

What is clear is that the format and techniques of classroom education are slow to change. Schools are currently expected to teach basic skills in reading, writing, mathematics, and reasoning. They are also supposed to introduce students to a complex cultural tradition in the liberal arts and the sciences, a tradition that now includes the entire world, not simply Western civilization.

They are further charged with developing individual skills relating to such nonacademic areas as vocation, leisure-time activity, and citizenship, as well as providing such specialised programs as driver education, sex education, drug education, and parent education.

By the 1970s apprehensions grew that American schools were not accomplishing all these objectives; indeed, the objectives themselves were questioned as possibly unreasonable.

In a famous research study, *Equality of Educational Opportunity* (1966), the American educator James Coleman (1926-95) concluded that family background had more impact than did school experience on many of the objectives that schools were attempting to achieve. Public concern and even pessimism about the educational and social impact of schools were reflected in the subsequent reluctance by taxpayers to approve additional expenditures for public education. The back-to-basics movement at the end of the 1970s was an early attempt by educators to narrow and sharpen their ambitions. Other efforts began in the 1980s to restore interest in academic quality.

During the late 1980s and early '90s some states sought far-reaching restructuring of education. In the most common strategy, reformers concentrated on statewide curriculum frameworks to specify what students should know and be able to do. Tests requiring essays, group work, and projects were planned to reveal whether students had mastered the curriculum. Even so, many people doubted the ability of public education to accomplish these goals; accordingly, interest in greater school choice increased.

Women in the Workforce

Abzug was the daughter of Russian-Jewish immigrants. She earned degrees from Hunter College of the City University of New York (B.A., 1942) and Columbia University Law School, New York City (LL.B., 1947). It was during her years as an attorney (1947-70), when few women were practicing law, that she began wearing her signature wide-brimmed hats to ensure that her clients and colleagues did not assume she was a secretary.

She acted as chief defense attorney for Willie McGee, an African-American man convicted and eventually executed for raping a white woman in Mississippi, defended victims of Sen. Joseph McCarthy's anticommunist witch-hunts, and helped draft legislation for the 1954 Civil Rights Act and the 1965 Voting Rights Act. To fight the U.S. government's plans to resume nuclear-weapons testing, she founded the Women Strike for Peace in 1961, and to protest the Vietnam War, she led the Democratic Party's "Dump Johnson" movement and supported Sen. Eugene McCarthy in his 1968 bid for the presidency. Along with Gloria Steinem and Betty Friedan, Abzug was in the forefront of the feminist movement and was an early advocate for equal rights for women, abortion rights, and child-care legislation.

She successfully ran for Congress in 1970 from Manhattan's 19th district with the slogan "This woman's place is in the House-the House of Representatives." On her first day in Congress (Jan. 21, 1971), she introduced a motion calling for the withdrawal of U.S. troops from

Vietnam, and she later used a little-known procedural tactic to force Pres.

Richard Nixon's administration to release the top-secret Pentagon Papers. She was also the first member of Congress to call for Nixon's impeachment. After serving three terms in the House, she lost a Senate race to Daniel P. Moynihan in 1977. Firmly committed to women's empowerment, she founded several organisations, including the National Women's Political Caucus and the International Women's Environment and Development Association, and she participated in the UN's Fourth World Conference on Women in 1995. For most of written history, agriculture was the chief human occupation, and heavy physical labour was not confined to men. Women performed backbreaking chores like grinding grain by hand in a stone quern, drawing and carrying water, gathering wood, and churning milk to make butter. About the only time women were given a respite was immediately before and after giving birth. With the Industrial Revolution the work situation changed for both men and women.

Whereas the hearth and home had formerly been the centre of production and family life, with industrialisation the factory became the workplace and the town the dwelling place. The role of women in the family work force did not change overnight, however, for at first whole families were employed in factories almost as teams. Not until the mid-19th century did the role of the male as the "good provider" emerge, with women relegated to household and domestic tasks. This was caused, perhaps, not so much by the change from farming to industrial technology as by a growing humanitarian protest against the harsh treatment of women and children in the early factory system. Legislation—most notably in Britain—raised the minimum age for child labour in factories, set limits on the working hours of women and children, and barred them from certain dangerous and heavy occupations.

Thus, more women were engaged primarily in domestic tasks and child care at home while the men went out to work. Being the sole wage earner in the family reinforced the man's traditional position as the head of the family, who was expected to direct the lives of his dependents.

Whatever authority the woman exercised derived from her status as mistress of the household. The tradition of the deferential female wedded to motherhood and domesticity persisted throughout the 19th century and well into the 20th. After the coming of electric power near the close of the 19th century, advances in technology brought labour-saving devices such as washing machines and vacuum cleaners into the home.

Although they changed the nature of some tasks and freed the housewife from some drudgery, they did little to lessen the amount of time she spent on household duties. At the same time that women's household work was being transformed by technology, changes were occurring in the economy and society leading to the growth of administrative and service jobs. The extension of public education created a demand for more teachers, and growing industrial and commercial enterprises required more office workers and salespeople.

While men could have—and earlier had—performed teaching and clerical tasks, it was discovered that it was cheaper to hire women for these occupations. The prevailing attitude was that, since men were the heads of households, they had to be paid enough to support a family. On the other hand, most women who entered the work force in the

United States before World War II were single and did not have families to support; hence, they could be paid lower wages. This inequality in men's and women's pay scales, even for equal work, still prevails. Technological changes affecting the maternal role of women also had an impact on their ability to leave the home. The development of contraceptive devices and the baby bottle and rubber nipple gave women greater freedom, making it easier for them to take outside jobs. Even if her employment was interrupted by childbirth, the woman could, within a relatively short time, reenter the work force. Many working women performed tasks closely related to their traditional household work.

When clothes were less often made at home but purchased ready-made at stores, for example, women were hired as seamstresses in the doming industry. Even after national emergencies such as the world wars, during which women were encouraged to take manufacturing jobs to replace the men who were in military service, women returned to housekeeping or to traditionally female occupations such as office work and nursing. In the 1970s married women began entering the labour force in great numbers, and the strict segregation of women into certain occupations began to lessen somewhat as new opportunities arose for female workers in traditionally male occupations.

New technology has meant that many tasks that once required heavy physical exertion, and hence were restricted to men, can now be performed simply by pushing buttons. Operating a bulldozer, for instance, does not need muscle power so much as alertness, judgment, and coordination—qualities as plentiful in women as in men.

Nevertheless, the entrance of women into occupations formerly the province of men proved to be slower than expected. This persistent occupational segregation by sex is largely responsible for sizable differences in rates of pay that still exist. It would appear that, although rapid technological progress has enabled women in highly industrialised nations to cast off certain traditional roles, technological determinism—or technological rationality—does not always prevail over cultural views and social practices inherited from the past. According to Marxist theory, the individual is heavily influenced by the structure of society, which in all modern societies mean a class structure; that is, people's opportunities, wants and interests are seen to be shaped by the mode of production that characterizes the society they inhabit.

Marxist feminists see contemporary gender inequality as determined ultimately by the capitalist mode of production. Gender oppression is class oppression and women's subordination is seen as a form of class oppression which is maintained (like racism) because it serves the interests of capital and the ruling class. Marxist feminists have extended traditional Marxist analysis by looking at domestic labour as well as wage work in order to support their position. Radical Women, a major Marxist-feminist organization, bases its theory on Marx' and Engels' analysis that the enslavement of women was the first building block of an economic system based on private property.

They contend that elimination of the capitalist profit-driven economy will remove the motivation for sexism, racism, homophobia and other forms of oppression. Gayle Rubin, who has written on a certain range of subjects including sadomasochism, prostitution, pornography and lesbian literature as well as anthropological studies and histories of sexual subcultures, first rose to prominence through her 1975 essay *"The Traffic in Women: Notes on the 'Political Economy' of Sex"*, in which she coins the phrase "sex/gender system" and criticizes Marxism for what she claims is its incomplete analysis of sexism under capitalism, without dismissing or dismantling Marxist fundamentals in the process.

It is worth mentioning that Radical feminism, which emerged in the 1970s, also took issue with Marxist feminism. Radical feminist theorists stated that modern society and its constructs (law, religion, politics, art, *etc*) are the product of males and therefore have a patriarchal character. According to those who subscribe to this view, the best solution for women's oppression would be to treat patriarchy not as a subset of capitalism but as a problem in its own right. Thus eliminating women's oppression means eliminating male domination in all its forms.

Like most feminists, however, radical feminists believe in replacing such domination with a culture and policy of equality. Austrian economist Ludwig von Mises argued against the Marxist account of the experience of women. He argued that the women's movement was an evolutionary, rather than revolutionary, step that furthered gains that capitalism had secured for women. He claimed to show that women gained along with the rise of classical liberalism. Under this analysis, the marriage contract was actually a first, albeit imperfect, step toward liberating women from the subservient position they had held since the age of violence. Proponents of Socialist feminism have also criticized the Marxist interpretation for failing to find an inherent connection between patriarchy and classism. Orthodox Marxists point out that most Marxist forerunners claimed by feminists or "marxist feminists" including Clara Zetkin and Alexandra Kollontai were against feminism. They agreed with the main Marxist movement that feminism was a bourgeois ideology counterposed to Marxism and against the working class. Instead of feminism the Marxists supported the more radical political program of liberating women through socialist revolution, with a special emphasis on work among women and in materially changing their conditions after the revolution.

It can be surmised from the foregoing discussion that womenpower is treated as secondary to manpower. Thus rose the feminst movement.

Here in this book we will try to elucidate various salient aspects of womenpower development. The text is supported by facts and findings of various eminent scholars in the field.

2

Development Process and Women

> "Remember that you are but an actor, acting whatever part the Master has ordained. It may be short or it may be long. If he wishes you to represent a poor man, do so heartily; if a cripple or magistrate, or a private man, in each case act your part with honour."
>
> —*Epictetus*

In the present chapter we intend to give an account of the issues of womenpower development.

Currently the world is passing through the worst crisis in its recent history. The production of the developing countries as a whole stagnated and per capita income declined during this period. The economic revival in the United States and Japan and some improvement in the economic situation in Western Europe did not trigger off revival in the developing countries as predicted.

The increased interest rates, combined with the rising exchange rate of the dollar and the growing debt burden, have led the developing countries to increase the supply of primary commodities in order to earn the foreign exchange needed to pay the debt obligations, which in turn brought a further deterioration of primary commodity markets. Market for manufactured products continues to be adversely affected by increased protectionist measures. Developing countries are forced to reduce their deficits in the balance of payments, while the cost of debt servicing is continually rising. The reduction of the deficit in balance of payments achieved by a drastic curtailment of imports, decreased rate of investments and reduced consumption is adversely affecting the economic growth of the developing countries, and thus their socioeconomic development, threatening the progressive trends during the last two decades.

Open and hidden unemployment is increasing, and so are poverty and human misery. The massive death toll precipitated by famines in Africa is the most pronounced expression of the severity of the present-day crisis. The devastating consequences of the world economic crisis have exacerbated the problem of women, as a component part of the general problems of developing countries. They have demonstrated that the position of women highlights the major problems of developing countries today. Since its inception, the Movement of the Non-Aligned countries, which encourage passes and represents the values and aspirations of an overwhelming majority of mankind, has been striving for the self-determination and emancipation of nations for equality among them, for a better life for each of our peoples, and for the improvement of the quality of the lives of men and women of all races and creeds, as was stressed by Late Indira Gandhi in her address to the Inaugural Session of the Seventh Conference of Heads of State or Government of the Non-Aligned Countries—Parallel to its struggle for political independence, self-determination and the sovereignty of all nations and for peace and cooperation on a basis of equality, the Movement has taken strong and consistent stand in favour of the kind of development which would benefit all countries, developing and developed alike.

Today, more than ever before, the world needs fundamental changes so that stable global development, as well as peace and security may be ensured. Ways out of the present crisis must be sought in a genuine democration of international relations.

Obviously, this implies, *inter alia* the elimination of all forms of the policy of force, domination, hegemony, discrimination, exploitation and inequality, of colonialism and neo-colonialism, the eradication of the abhorrent system of apartheid, racism, foreign domination and aggression, intervention, interference in the internal affairs of states, occupation and pressures.

It also involves the acceleration of the process of self-determination of peoples under colonial and alien domination, the consolidation of national independence, sovereignty and territorial integrity of states, as well as the halting of the arms race in order to enable the enormous material and human resources wasted by the arms race to be used for the economic and social development of all countries. In fact, role of women in development is most intimately related to the goal of comprehensive socio-economic development, and is a strategic question for the development of all societies.

Any development strategy which neglects the need for enhancing the role of women cannot lead to comprehensive socio-economic development. The point of departure is to 'recognise the role of women as a dynamic factor and a valuable asset for the overall process of development—it is not a burden or cost nor a mere humanitarian concession to a disadvantaged group. The scattered, piecemeal or curative approaches to the advancement of women view women as passive subjects of protection or as recipients of marginal welfare and social services, unrelated to policies and strategies for economic development or to structural changes in societies that result form economic changes.

Such approaches have failed to prevent the growing marginalisation of women in the economy and in the political process in most developing, and even developed countries. In the absence of an integrated approach to development, a fragmentary approach to the position of women in development has been perpetuated and has led to the unsatisfactory option of promoting the advancement of women by social welfare, humanitarian and demographic approaches, without due attention to the transformations needed to create conditions in which women can unfold their full potential as a factor of development.

These approaches should now be replaced by an integrated and participatory approach which relates the role of women in development, their aspirations and needs to the critical areas, issues and choices in the developmental strategy for economic growth, a more humane use of material and human resources, and for equity in power relations at the national and international levels. The position of women and their role in this context are particularly important, not only because women constitute half of the human resources in developing countries, but also because they have to bear the brunt of the daily struggle for survival in developing countries.

Although women are not a homogenous social group, and their position varies between and within countries, there are some features which are common to all societies. Historically their role in biological reproduction has generally restricted women's participation in the mainstream of social, economic and political processes.

Processes of change in women's position depend

primarily on the interrelations between transformative factors and forces, spontaneous of consciously directed, and the inherited matrix of social and cultural institutions, values, norms and practices, forms of prod action and distribution.

These are manifested in the division of resources, labour and power. In most developing societies, colonialism brought about major structural changes affecting people's access to and control over resources and power relations within and outside the communities and also the distribution of the roles and responsibilities of both men and women. After the attainment of independendence, wherever narrow economic growth-oriented models were adopted, the distortions and imbalances prevailing under the colonial regimes tended to continue. As a result, substantial sections of the population, which were already under 'various pressures and handicaps, became even more marginalised.

The request for equality for women received a considerable boost from two sources. First, in the struggle against colonialism and in the national liberation wars men and women had joined hands on terms of equality as members of one human family. Secondly, as a result of the World War II the concept of the equality of the sexes as one of the basic principles on which a community should be based was incorporated in the UN Charter, and with this first received global recognition. The nonaligned and other developing countries have strongly supported the recommendations of the World Conference on the International Women's Year in Mexico in 1975, and the World Conference of the UN Decade for Women in Copenhagen in 1980, on the role of women in development, and further elaborated the common strategy to spend up their economic and social progress and promote the efforts towards the establishment of the New International Economic Order. Experience acquired during the UN Decade for Women; Equality, Development and Peace (1976-1985) has indicated how the process of development can be promoted or constrained by the integration or non-integration of the productive, reproductive and household functions of women into development processes.

The Decade has increased the general awareness of the continued violations of the basic rights and needs of women. It has also contributed to the knowledge of the role of women in development, reflecting the developmental dimension of the problem and stimulating farther along those lines at the national and internationals. The review and evaluation of the progress in this field particularly at the mid-point of the Third UN Development Decade ana at the end of the UN Decade for Women, indicate—that some positive changes have been achieved, particularly in providing some basic preconditions for the integration of women into development processes. Almost all countries have improved their legislative systems and have taken measures towards eliminating *dejure* discrimination against women; the educational level—including that of women—has risen, health conditions have improved, as indicated, for example, by the life expectancy statistics, expansion of industry and services have created more employment opportunities, there has been some improvement in rural areas, social services and infrastructure have expanded, etc.

However, available data indicate that these improvements have been of only relative value in some countries improvements have been slow and the recent economic crisis has slowed down the positive trends in many countries or even reversed them. An aggregate analysis of the most characteristic indicators in the fields defined as the sub-themes of the World Conference on the UN Decade for Women—employment, health and education—shows mixed picture of achievement in the past which does not live up to the expectations, both in terms of decreasing the disparities between men and women in the group of developing countries, on the one hand, and the disparities between the developed and developing countries, on the other.

In the last few years, not only has the position of the developing countries in world economic relations considerably deteriorated but the solution of the problems of the world economy is being attempted at the expense of these countries, particularly of the most depressed strata of their societies, including women. There is also evidence to suggest that, despite legislative steps, prejudices, traditional attitudes and practices continue to perpetuate discrimination against women. Evidence shows that the process of marginalisation of women in development has been intensified by the current processes of economic change and may continue in the future.

The marginal position of a large section of society, and specifically women, can no longer be justified. The structural changes in the economies of developing countries which are likely to follow future developments in science and technology must be based on increased and genuine participation of all members to society, if they are not to result in still greater imbalances or even lead to disaster. The role of women in overall development has not been fully understood, nor has it been given its full weight in the struggle to eliminate poverty, hunger, inequality and injustice at the national as well as the international level.

The continued assumption that the responsibility for

childrearing and for family needs lies with women alone, as well as the persistence of intra-household inequalities, place severe strains on women's health, limit their capacity to participate efficiently in the production process and further jeopardize their chances for a fair share in the benefits of society. It is thus becoming overwhelmingly clear that in searching for solutions to these contradictions the inequalities between men and women have to be examined from a developmental perspective. On the one hand, the concerns of relevance to women cannot be resolved automatically through economic growth alone. On the other hand, egalitarian processes and policy action to improve women's position within developing countries are only a necessary but not a sufficient condition to increase the quality of life of the women in these countries, particularly in view of the grave consequences of the world economic crisis.

Simultaneous and concerted action is necessary to improve the conditions for growth and development by appropriate domestic and international policies, articulating within that developmental framework measures to enhance the role and position of women as a factor of development. In spite of the fact that women in developing countries are massively involved in key areas of production, such as agriculture, food production, trade, etc., their work is not fully recognised and valued. The activities of women as producers are usually not adequately included in statistics, thus making their contribution invisible.

They usually do not have adequate access to the factors of production, to land, credit and other tools io raise their productivity—i.e., appropriate scientific and technical information, training and other policy support. If the crucial problems of the contemporary world are viewed in their relationship and interdependence, the questions related to the role of women in development opportunities for the growing population, to solve the demographic problems, to secure basic needs and services, such as food, education, health housing, to establish the role of the informal sector of the economy, to approach and solve migration problems, to equip and prepare the human resources of tomorrow to face the challenges to the 21st century, to ascertain the impact of the frontier technologies, such as communications, microelectronics bioengineering, biotechnology, and to protect the environment.

The research undertaken during the UN Decade for Women has articulated the critical connections between these developmental issues and the role and status of women— as beneficiaries or victims, active agents or passive sufferers, and demonstrates the necessity of the full integration of women into development efforts in both developing and developed countries. The two facets of the role of women—in production and reproduction should be conceived as complementary and interactive.

In order to release women's potentials for fuller participation in the productive and decision-making processes, there is a need not only for a sharing of parental responsibilities but also for institutional provisions which would benefit children and families. Women should have the right, the requisite knowledge and the resources to regulate their reproductive capacity. However, without economic independence women cannot achieve equality. Therefore, measures to expand satisfactory employment opportunities, to improve their economic status and the provision of the necessary infrastructure should be treated as an important and integral part of national and international development strategies.

The short term policies and emergency measures introduced for the management of the economy in the context of the present crisis should not distort the long-term objectives of development and prevent the social transformation, of which the integration of women in development is an indispensable clement. The non-aligned and other developing countries have emphasised that development can be achieved only through maximum participation of both men and women, in all spheres and at all levels of life, work and decision making—in the priority-setting, design and implementation of measures for change. Such active participation constitutes the basic ingredient of the strategy for individual and collective self-reliance of developing countries. The policy of individual and collective self-reliance provides an appropriate framework for the search for such development approaches, since it is based on the sovereign rights of states to control and develop their natural and human resources, and promote international cooperation, on the basis of equality and mutual assistance. By mobilising their own resources and the masses of the population and developing their collective self-reliance, the developing countries contribute to the establishment of new economic relations for the common good.

The non-aligned and other developing countries are investing considerable efforts in the establishment of mutual links, especially in those fields where cooperation could speed up development, through a number of areas of economic cooperation, as well as through various other forms of economic and technical co-operation which have been particularly supported by the Group of 77. However, the role of women as a factor of development has rarely been taken into consideration in the designing and practical implementation of the projects for economic and technical cooperation among developing countries.

It is becoming increasingly clear that concept of integrated development and the sustained elaboration and integration of the role of women as a factor of development—through coordinated activity of the non-aligned and other developing countries supported by the United Nations and other international organisations—could contribute to a better adaptation of the economic and technical cooperation among the developing countries to the concrete conditions and actual needs of the people. In fact, an insight is needed into the institutional mechanisms that promote or prevent changes and transformations in individual sectors or areas of social and economic life.

It should, however, be kept in mind that the harmonisation of women's productive, reproductive and participatory roles cannot be achieved at the individual level. The interlinkages among sectors and areas are therefore crucial when general development concepts are operationalised through development planning, development of human resources, employment, technological and scientific change etc. The sectors and areas included here have been chosen because of their relevance for the advancement of women.

Some relevant areas, such as employment, have been treated within all sectors. The measures proposed in relation to specific sectoral issues influence other sectors and institutions, and thus have a synergetic development effect. This is especially so in the case of science and technology. The transfer of technology from developed to developing countries influences the organisation of the production process in all economic sectors, and affects all other socio-economic spheres.

3

Strategies

"Reform is sometimes so eager to do good,
it tries to right wrongs that do not exist."

Women constitute half of the total human population, hence there is huge potential of womenpower. Unfortunately this could not be tapped. Only recently we have realised their role from home-maker to excellent top managers.

As we intend to present various strategies for womenpower development, it is necessary few concepts of empowerment and development and their application to realising the intended goal.

First we will address feminism. In fact, the term Feminism can be used to describe a political, cultural or economic movement aimed at establishing more rights and legal protection for women. Feminism involves political and sociological theories and philosophies concerned with issues of gender difference, as well as a movement that advocates more gender-specific rights for women and campaigns for women's rights and interests.

Although the terms "feminism" and "feminist" did not gain widespread use until the 1970s, they were already being used in the public parlance much earlier. According to Maggie Humm and Rebecca Walker, the history of feminism can be divided into three waves. The first feminist wave was in the nineteenth and early twentieth centuries, the second was in the 1960s and 1970s, and the third extends from the 1990s to the present.

Feminist theory emerged from these feminist movements. It is manifest in a variety of disciplines such as feminist geography, feminist history and feminist literary criticism. Remarkably, feminism has altered predominant perspectives in a wide range of areas within Western society, ranging from culture to law. Feminist activists have campaigned for women's legal rights (rights of contract, property rights, voting rights); for women's right to bodily integrity and autonomy, for abortion rights, and for reproductive rights (including access to contraception and quality prenatal care); for protection of women and girls from domestic violence, sexual harassment and rape; for workplace rights, including maternity leave and equal pay; against misogyny; and against other forms of gender-specific discrimination against women. Feminism has thus far failed to add equal rights for women to the United States Constitution.

During much of its history, most feminist movements and theories had leaders who were predominantly middle-class white women from Western Europe and North America. However, at least since Sojourner Truth's 1851 speech to American feminists, women of other races have proposed alternative feminisms. This trend accelerated in the 1960s with the Civil Rights movement in the United States and the collapse of European colonialism in Africa, the Caribbean, parts of Latin America and Southeast Asia.

Since that time, women in former European colonies and the Third World have proposed "Post-colonial" and

"Third World" feminisms. Some Postcolonial Feminists, such as Chandra Talpade Mohanty, are critical of Western feminism for being ethnocentric. Black feminists, such as Angela Davis and Alice Walker, share this view. Feminists and scholars have divided the movement's history into three "waves".

The First Wave Feminism

In fact, First-wave feminism refers to an extended period of feminist activity during the nineteenth century and early twentieth century in the United Kingdom and the United States. Originally it focused on the promotion of equal contract and property rights for women and the opposition to chattel marriage and ownership of married women (and their children) by their husbands. However, by the end of the nineteenth century, activism focused primarily on gaining political power, particularly the right of women's suffrage.

Yet, feminists such as Voltairine de Cleyre and Margaret Sanger were still active in campaigning for women's sexual, reproductive, and economic rights at this time. In 1854, Florence Nightingale established female nurses as adjuncts to the military. In Britain the Suffragettes and, possibly more effectively, the Suffragists campaigned for the women's vote. In 1918 the Representation of the People Act 1918 was passed granting the vote to women over the age of 30 who owned houses. In 1928 this was extended to all women over twenty-one. In the United States, leaders of this movement included Lucretia Mott, Lucy Stone, Elizabeth Cady Stanton, and Susan B. Anthony, who each campaigned for the abolition of slavery prior to championing women's right to vote; all were strongly influenced by Quaker thought.

American first-wave feminism involved a wide range

of women. Some, such as Frances Willard, belonged to conservative Christian groups such as the Woman's Christian Temperance Union.

Others, such as Matilda Joslyn Gage, were more radical, and expressed themselves within the National Woman Suffrage Association or individually. American first-wave feminism is considered to have ended with the passage of the Nineteenth Amendment to the United States Constitution (1919), granting women the right to vote in all states. The term *first wave* was coined retrospectively after the term *second-wave feminism* began to be used to describe a newer feminist movement that focused as much on fighting social and cultural inequalities as political inequalities.

The Second Wave Feminism

Second-wave feminism refers to the period of activity in the early 1960s and lasting through the late 1980s. The scholar Imelda Whelehan suggests that the second wave was a continuation of the earlier phase of feminism involving the suffragettes in the UK and USA. Second-wave feminism has continued to exist since that time and coexists with what is termed *third-wave feminism.* The scholar Estelle Freedman compares first and second-wave feminism saying that the first wave focused on rights such as suffrage, whereas the second wave was largely concerned with other issues of equality, such as ending discrimination. The feminist activist and author Carol Hanisch coined the slogan "The Personal is Political" which became synonymous with the second wave.

Second-wave feminists saw women's cultural and political inequalities as inextricably linked and encouraged women to understand aspects of their personal lives as deeply politicized and as reflecting sexist power structures.

It is significant to note that the French author and philosopher Simone de Beauvoir wrote novels; monographs on philosophy, politics, and social issues; essays; biographies; and an autobiography. She is now best known for her metaphysical novels, including *She Came to Stay* and *The Mandarins*, and for her treatise *The Second Sex*, a detailed analysis of women's oppression and a foundational tract of contemporary feminism. Written in 1949, its English translation was published in 1953. It sets out a feminist existentialism which prescribes a moral revolution.

As an existentialist, she accepted Jean-Paul Sartre's precept *existence precedes essence*; hence "one is not born a woman, but becomes one." Her analysis focuses on the social construction of Woman as the Other. This de Beauvoir identifies as fundamental to women's oppression. She argues women have historically been considered deviant and abnormal and contends that even Mary Wollstonecraft considered men to be the ideal toward which women should aspire. De Beauvoir argues that for feminism to move forward, this attitude must be set aside. Betty Friedan's *The Feminine Mystique* (1963) criticized the idea that women could only find fulfillment through childrearing and homemaking. According to Friedan's obituary in the *The New York Times*, *The Feminine Mystique* "ignited the contemporary women's movement in 1963 and as a result permanently transformed the social fabric of the United States and countries around the world" and "is widely regarded as one of the most influential nonfiction books of the 20th century."

In the book Friedan hypothesizes that women are victims of a false belief system that requires them to find identity and meaning in their lives through their husbands and children. Such a system causes women to completely lose their identity in that of their family. Friedan specifically locates this system among post-World War II middle-class suburban communities. At the same time, America's post-war economic boom had led to the development of new technologies that were supposed to make household work less difficult, but that often had the result of making women's work less meaningful and valuable. The phrase "Women's Liberation" was first used in the United States in 1964 and first appeared in print in 1966. By 1968, although the term *Women's Liberation Front* appeared in the magazine *Ramparts*, it was starting to refer to the whole women's movement. Bra-burning also became associated with the movement, though the actual prevalence of bra-burning is debatable.

One of the most vocal critics of the women's liberation movement has been the African American feminist and intellectual Gloria Jean Watkins (who uses the pseudonym "bell hooks") who argues that this movement glossed over race and class and thus failed to address "the issues that divided women."

The Third Wave Feminism

Remarkably, Third-wave feminism began in the early 1990s, arising as a response to perceived failures of the second wave and also as a response to the backlash against initiatives and movements created by the second wave. Third-wave feminism seeks to challenge or avoid what it deems the second wave's essentialist definitions of femininity, which (according to them) over-emphasize the experiences of upper middle-class white women. A post-structuralist interpretation of gender and sexuality is central to much of the third wave's ideology.

Third-wave feminists often focus on "micro-politics"

and challenge the second wave's paradigm as to what is, or is not, good for females. The third wave has its origins in the mid-1980s.

Feminist leaders rooted in the second wave like Gloria Anzaldua, bell hooks, Chela Sandoval, Cherrie Moraga, Audre Lorde, Maxine Hong Kingston, and many other black feminists, sought to negotiate a space within feminist thought for consideration of race-related subjectivities. Third-wave feminism also contains internal debates between difference feminists such as the psychologist Carol Gilligan (who believes that there are important differences between the sexes) and those who believe that there are no inherent differences between the sexes and contend that gender roles are due to social conditioning.

Empowerment

Now it is necessary to understand empowerment in the context of womenpower. Empowerment is a multi-dimensional process which should enable individuals or a group of individuals to realise their full identity and powers in all spheres of life. It consist of greater access to knowledge and resources, greater autonomy in decision making to enable them to have greater ability to plan their lives, or have greater control over the circumstances that influence their lives and free them from shackles imposed on them by custom, belief and practice.

Generally, development with justice is expected to generate the forces that lead to empowerment of various sections of population in a country and to raise their status. Discrimination of women from *womb to tomb* is well known. The National Perspective Plans for Women 1988-2000 A.D. (1988) which has made a free, frank, objective and masterly analysis of the impact of developmental plans and programmes of Indian women, with special reference to Rural Women, gives us the following profile of women in India.

"There is continued inequality and vulnerability of women in all sectors—economic, social, political, educational health care, nutrition and legal."

The Main indicators:	
Women illiterates	Over 75%
Rural illiterate women	83%
Women, working in unorganised sectors	Over 90%
Of these unskilled labour in agriculture and construction	83%
Women having full time employment in organised sectors	14%
Maternity benefits and child care available in organised sectors	3.5%
Registered unemployed school graduates	51 lakhs
Pregnant women who are anaemic	65%
Infant mortality rate (in the first year of birth)	10%
Of which in slum areas	12.4%
Children dying because of malnutrition before the age of 5 years	40%
Sex ratio—933 females to every 100 males	
Expectation of life at birth—51.6 as against 5.26 for males property owned by women less than	1%

On an average a rural women works for 18 hours a day.

Recent happenings opposed to women's rights to equality and freedom are—renewal of widow immolation opposition to a divorced women's right to maintenance, resistence to prohibitions of dowry, rapid rise of crimes of violence against women—rape, murder, infanticide, foeticide, Projection of women in the media as sex objects, man eaters or long suffering martyrs accepting humiliation and illtreatment, glamourising their powerlessness,

(1) The problems of women are well defined.

(2) What is the cause of her powerlessness? Herself? Her nature?

(3) Is she inherently weaker?

(4) Is she a parasite?

(5) Does she naturally need a support?

(6) Is her femaleness the cause of all trouble?

It is pertinent to note that there is a lot of confusion in people's mind regarding nature the inborn traits of women and nurture, the socialisation process that makes here what she becomes. There is also confusion between sex, i.e. (femaleness and maleness) and gender, the role of male or i.e. female as perceived in society. The root cause of women's oppression is patriarchy which has snatched legitimate powers form women, making them totally defenceless and powerless. Hence women need to be empowered not as a favour to them but for undoing the injustice meted out to them. Soviet President, Mikhail Gorbachev, in his welcome address to the World Congress of Women at Moscow in June 1987 said, "The Status of Women is a barometer of the democratism of any State, an indicator of how human rights are respected in it." As women are oppressed in all spheres of life, they need to be empowered in all walks of life.

There cannot be a piecemeal approach to women's empowerment. Hence all aspects of society have to be restructured. Basically, empowerment is an active process. Power is not a commodity to be transacted. Power cannot be given away as alms. Power has to be acquired. Once acquired, it needs to be exercised, sustained and preserved. Women have to empower themselves.

No doubt, as a corrective measure Governments may offer welfare schemes for women. They may float anti-poverty programmes. They may launch projects for their uplift. They may enact legislation to safeguard women's rights. The Government policies can only facilitate the process, reduce the hurdles and create an atmosphere conducive to transformation.

But it is the women who have to empower themselves. Unless they themselves become conscious of their oppression, show initiative and seize the opportunities, it would not be possible to change their status.

It is apt to quote Nehru who said—"To awaken the people, it is women who must be awakened; once she is on the move, the family moves, the village moves and the nation moves."

Basically, empowerment mechanism is easily enumerated. But the question is the operationalisation. Unanimously, the women should have:

(a) better care of health for herself and her children

(b) higher literacy and education

(c) higher age at marriage

(d) acceptance of a small family norm

(e) greater work participation in modernised sector

(f) self-reliance, self-respect and dignity among women

(g) better consciousness of their rights

(h) higher standard of living

(i) no dependence on males etc.

Let us empower our own students, first, by

(a) removing sex bias in our curriculum and by designing courses incorporating women's dimensions.

(b) emphasising on the multiple role of women.

(c) developing the ability to think creatively about situations the hurdles to face, possibilities of change, the coping mechanism etc.

(d) overcoming social taboos and traditional beliefs.

(e) encouraging late marriages.

(f) sensitising them to laws related to property, marriage, divorce, minimum wages, maternity leave benefit etc.

(g) making them aware of possibilities of self-employment.

(h) helping them to develop interest in application of science.

(i) encouraging them to take careers seriously.

(j) encouraging to believe in their own ability and a sense self-worth.

(k) educating parents on the importance of making women economically self-sufficient.

Development tasks connected with health care, environmental safety, promotion of population, education activities, family welfare, citizenship roles and responsibilities, legal rights, drudgery reduction, combating atrocities and violences committed to women, etc. could be taken up in our community service, social service and adult education activities. Let us, through our extension activities, get our students to take up action programmes to raise the consciousness of rural women and empower them.

Women and Education

We have ample evidence to prove that co-education existed in the Ashramas. But as conditions changed, when girls started to lose the privileges of education, the marriage age came down, they lost their equality, came to be considered as mere possessions and by 100 A.D. i.e. Manu's time, they were ascribed completely to a dependent status. This law giver has said, "By a girl, by a young women, or even by an aged, nothing must be done independently even in her own home." The most noteworthy feature of ancient Indian Education is the education of women. Women were given equal rights with men in all walks of life, including education. Ladies have been quoted as authors of some of the samhitas of *Rig Veda.* We here of lady philosophers and Brahma Vadinis who dedicated their whole lives to education. We find that women had the freedom to remain single as well as freedom to chose their life partners.

During the middle ages, seclusion of "Purdah," was added to the existing subordinate and subservient status of women and in course of time, women became completely illiterate and entirely dependant on men-father, husband and son, economically, socially and culturally.

All over the world, the movement for improving women's status has always emphasised education as the most significant instrument for social change. The social reformers of the 19th Century tried to use education more to ameliorate the position of women socially; they were able to awaken the consciousness of the nation to the evils of child marriage, sati, polygamy, enforced widowhood, dowry system etc. Since the new western education which developed during the 19th Century invariably meant "a method of earning" and since women were not required to earn, it was not considered necessary for women to be educated. Learning to do household work was sufficient for her and so the parents were not keen to incur any expenditure in educating the girls till very recently.

During the twentieth century, the country has made spectacular progress in promoting the interests of women. The literacy rate went up form about 7% in 1901 to 7.9% in 1951. 18% in 1971. 24.88% in 1981 and 39.63% in 1991. But there is still a wide gap between male and female literacy. Among the males the corresponding rise is from 24.9% to 46.7% i.e. the gap in percentage literacy points between male and female literacy has increased from 17 in 1951 to 22 in 1981. In absolute terms too, the number of illiterate women has increased during this period from 158.7 million to 241.7 million in 1981 and to 352 million in 1991. Women comprised 57% of the illiterate population in 1981 and 45% in 1991; girls formed 70% of non-enrolled children in 1981, 60% in 1991 in the school age group. Three fourths of the 50 million children who are not enrolled in any school are girls.

It is estimated that 30% of the total work of fuel gathering, fetching water and farm work is done by girls between 6 and 11 years. Almost the entire burden of sibling care is on the girls child. In 1951, enrolment of boys in the primary stage was 55% of the population in the correspondingly age group and among girls, enrolment was only 20.1%. At the middle stage, 4.6% girls enrolled as against 20.8% of boys. At the secondary stage, for every 100 boys, only 16 girls enrolled. Enrolment of women in university education was about 11 for every 100 men. In 1981, for every 100 boys, the number of girls enrolled in the primary stage is 64, middle stage is 51, secondary stage is 31, university stage is 30 and vocational technical education is 20.

The male-female gaps have narrowed to a certain extent but girls are behind in numbers and the type of education. In 1991, 42% of the pupils enrolled at primary school are girls and only 33% are enrolled in secondary school. Though the number of schools has increased phenomenally, in classes I to V, (age-group 6-11 years) one out of every three girls is still outside the school. The dropout rates for girls is very high, one out of every three girls is still outside the school. Of every 100 girls in Class I, only 30 each Class V. In Class VI-VIII (age group 11.-14 years) only 27 out of every 100 girls are at school as compared to 54 boys in this age group. At the secondary stage : i.e. Classes IX to XII, (in the age group 14-17 years) only 20 out of every hundred girls are in school as against 39 boys. Girls form less than one third of the total enrolment at the secondary level.

In fact, Girls' position is worse in vocational, professional and other special schools at the secondary levels. Girls go in only for female sex-typed courses such as nursing, teacher training, home science, music etc. and very few girls enrol in technical courses leading to industry. Female enrolment in higher education has gone up more than thirty points since 1951, the proportion of women to every hundred men at the University stage has increased from 14 to 46 in the past 36 years. But a large number of girls opt for general Arts and Humanities courses. In 1981, of every 100 girls enrolled, 56 were in Arts, 21 in Science, 13 in Commerce 7 in Engineering and 3.6 in Medicine. The number of women, per 100 men, faculty wise, was 60.5 in Arts, 40.4 in Science, 19.2 in Commerce, 91.9 in Education, 4 in Engineering and Technical Education, 32.5 in Medicine, 2.6 in Agriculture and 7.4 in Law. By 1987, enrolment of girls in Engineering increased by three times and in Medicine, one and a half times. There is uneven rate of progress of all levels of education not only between states but between different levels of education in the same state. There is vast disparity between education of girls in rural areas and urban areas. There is a big gap between enrolment of girls belonging to the scheduled caste/tribe and other castes.

Girls belonging to scheduled caste and tribes are also lagging behind boys belonging to SC/ST. The pattern of women's participation in the labour force can indicate women's education in preparing them for participation in national development on equal terms with men. We find the work participation rate of women is low in India, has declined from 33.7% in 1911 to 20.85% in 1981 the corresponding rate of male work participation in 1981 being 52.7%. If we look at the distribution of workers by individual category, 80% of the women workers are engaged in agriculture, 13% in organised sector of the economy and the rest in unorganised non-agricultural occupations. Of these women workers, more than 89% are illiterate, about 50% of the total 'non-working' women are engaged in household activities, hardly 0.2% are women in independent means. Even in the administrative services like IAS, IPS, where there is no sex-discrimination, hardly 7.5% are women. In 1988, there were 339 women IAS officers, out of a total of 4548. The Indian Forest Service has only 10 women officers i.e. 0.6% and in the IPS, there were 21 women officers as against 2418 men. The proportion of seats won by women to the Lok Sabha was 46 out of 537 seats. The Rajya Sabha had 28 women in a home of 245 seats. The pattern is similar at the State level. The incidence of unemployment also is high in that, they account for 40% of the total unemployment, which is higher than their share in the labour force which is 33%. The wage differentials between men and women continue to exist in spite of legislation enacted for "equal pay for equal work."

It is also found that women are predominantly employed in consumption linked services and not in production linked industrial occupations. Female workers are concentrated in unskilled, low status, low prestige, dead end jobs such as midwives, health visitors, clerks, teachers, unskilled office workers, food preservers, canners, nurses etc. Thus we can see that women are hurdled at the lowest occupational structure of the modern sector and the males continue to dominate the top echelons. Studies also show that mechanisation and modernisation have marginalised women in many sectors.

They are being pushed down or out of the work force. The average hours of unpaid work done by women outside their homes in rural areas vary from 6 to 7 hours a day. But their access to ownership of land and other productive resources remains negligible. 30 to 35% of the rural household are headed by women due to male migration or abandonment. Women comprise only 7.5% of the membership of registered trade unions, hardly one per cent being office bearers. Representation of women in elected offices has remained stagnant, inspite of the increased voting turn out in general election. Age specific death rates indicate higher rates for female child. The fertility rate has not declined to the desired extent, the average number of children born to a woman in her lifetime being 4.6. More than half of the women do not get sufficient dietary intake of calories, proteins, calcium, iron, vitamin A.

Two thirds of the pregnant women are anaemic, crimes against women continue unabated. There is resistance to prohibition of dowry. The projection of women in the media as sex objects, man eaters, or long suffering martyrs, accepting humiliation and illtreatment glamourise their powerlessness.

The expectation of life at birth was 52.9% years in 1981 and it has risen from 44.7 years in 1961. In 1991 it has risen to 55.9 years, equal to that of man.

The sex ratio has registered a slight increase, from 930 women per 1000 males in 1971 to 933 in 1981. But in 1991 it has come down to 927 females for every 1000 males.

The average age at marriage has reached 18.3 years in 1981 as against 17.1 in 1971.

The focus in the programmes for women has shifted from welfare to development and empowerment.

The cause of her powerlessness?
Herself or her nature?
Is she inherently weaker?
Is she a parasite?
Does she naturally need a support?
Is her femaleness the cause of all trouble?

There is a lot of confusion in people's mind regarding nature i.e. the inborn traits of women and nature, i.e., the socialisation process that makes her what she is. There is also confusion between sex i.e. femaleness and maleness and gender i.e. the role of a male or female as perceived in the society. The root cause of women's oppression is patriarchy, which has snatched legitimate powers from women, making them totally defenceless and powerless.

Hence women need to be empowered for undoing the

injustice meted out to them. Empowerment is an active, multi-dimensional process which should enable women to realise their full indentity and powers in all spheres of life. It would consist of greater access to knowledge and resources, greater autonomy in decision making, greater ability to plan their lives, have greater control over the circumstances that influence their lives and free them from shackles imposed on them by custom, belief and practice.

Generally, development with justice is expected to generate the forces that lead to empowerment of various sections of population in a country and to raise their status. But, power is not a commodity to be transacted. Power cannot be given away as alms. Power has to be acquired and once acquired, it needs to be exercised, sustained and preserved. Women have to empower themselves. Unless they themselves become conscious of their oppression, show initiative and seize the opportunities, it would not be possible to change their status in society.

The empowerment mechanism is easily enumerated

(a) better health care for herself and her children

(b) higher literacy and education

(c) higher age at marriage

(d) greater work participation in modernised sector

(e) necessary financial and service support

(g) advancement into higher position of power

(g) better consciousness of their rights

(h) self-reliance, self-respect and dignity among women

Education was for long disassociated from the idea of nation building. It was viewed as a process for infusing piety, during the ancient period. It was then seen as a cultural process, to transmit the accumulated wealth of knowledge, to impart classical values, and to build character of the individual. It was essentially for a privileged few and hence was not really contributory to the development of the nation as we understand today.

When the demand for women's education started in the 18th century, it was more in the light of women's rights, for the access to knowledge and not as a national economic asset. Then the attitude changed and for the first time, the UNESCO Conference in 1962 underlined the importance of the access of girls and women to technical and vocational education for economic and social development. According to Gunnar Myrdal (1969), education has an independent as well "instrumental" value, i.e. the purpose of education must be to rationalise attitude as well as to impart knowledge and skills. Education for national development should include education for self-reliance, personal development, social development, productive capacity, social integration and political understanding. Do we educate our girls for such an integrated development? What type of education should we plan? What type of curriculum should we develop to train the intellect, to discipline the emotions for social advancement and for creative contribution of our girls?

Is it enough to merely train he for her future career as wife and mother? Shall we continue the present system where the girls are educated merely to obtain a degree which is a passport to matrimony? Or, should we educate her according to her aptitude and ability and help her to attain the fullest possible development in all respects, personally, socially and economically and thus lead a complete life? The Indian constitution has guaranteed "Equal rights and equal opportunities to all its citizens, irrespective of sex, age, race or religion." The rights are guaranteed by law, but yet to be legalised in custom.

The International Conference on public education convened jointly by UNESCO and the International Bureau of Education, in Geneva 1952, while discussing the question of access of women to education, made the following recommendations to ministries of education of all member countries.

1. Every person, without distinction of sex should enjoy all the rights and freedom proclaimed by the "Universal Declaration of Human Rights," and that such equality should apply in all fields, particularly that of education.
2. Every person, man or woman should be able to receive an education enabling him to develop his aptitude as fully as possible, playing an effective part as member or citizen of his community, his nation and the world and meet the demands of his special tasks in life.
3. Women, like men should have opportunities to fulfil the tasks appropriate to the aptitudes.
4. General education should be equal in value and status of that of boys and thus avoid social discrimination.

No doubt, the constitution has granted social and political equality; perhaps India is the first country which decided on adult suffrage at the start of a parliamentary democracy and gave the rights to women at the same time as men. Political franchise extended to women would become meaningless if they are not able to understand the issues their votes are to decide. Social equality is practised by millions of women who have come out of their seclusion, a few pockets of orthodoxy still continues to react. Basically, in the sphere of economic activity very few women have developed the ability to stand on their own feet and be completely independent, majority of women follow merely the profession of matrimony and remain dependent on men.

Women have to be trained for economic emancipation. The participation of women in social, economic, political and cultural life would decide the country's advancement and success.

Need of Career Training

It is pertinent to note that all over the world, education is being reshaped for the following reasons. More and more linkages are being developed between education and work; there is a great concern for the rising rates of youth employment. There is a great need to create a labour force which would be capable of working in the growing complexity of technological application; proper attitudes and skills for employability have to be developed among the youth; there is a shift in proportion of women leaving the home and entering the work force. All these points to the need for an adequate programme of career guidance for the school leavers.

There should be increased access for women to vocational, technical and professional education and to the existing and emergent technologies. The choice of disciplines offered to women at all levels in all types of technical education should be in keeping with the objective of bringing about women's equality. The identification of some skills and occupation as "suitable" or "relevant" to women should no longer dictate the choice of subjects. The selection of subject should be based on the aptitude of the individual and the employment potential.

Adequate counselling services should be made available to all the students. The most serious omission in conceptualising career choice is the consideration of the effects of sex role socialisation on the decision making process. Career choices and career decisions are influenced by the decisions about marriage, parenthood, female-male responsibilities in home making etc. Social norms and expected sex roles also have an impact on career decision. Women are really not free to emplore their interest and make choices with a more conscious perspective. Girls capabilities are usually under estimated by the parents, teachers, and the society.

Indian girls have not been trained adequately by the educational institutions to be able to battle on their own and hence they give way to pressure and thus we find a vast number of able women ending up in low status, low paid jobs. Again, in a conservative society like India, aiming high in the external world of success and power by women is not relished. Usually, girls are not taken seriously as carrists as career is considered to be of secondary importance.

Notably, marriage is the main determinant of a woman's social position and it is more important to get married to men with high paid jobs. The traditional myth such as—girls do not need to work, the husband's duty is to support them, women's work is in the house, and those who work outside neglect their homes and children; women may work until they marry; married women and mothers are not reliable workers; women are poor at qualitative analysis and unable to make though decisions etc.—continue to influences women's career and act as barrier to women's advancement into senior positions.

If girls' careers are to be taken seriously the significance of subjects like Science and Mathematics should be explained to them in the middle school itself. Guidance should be given to them at the school stage itself for developing self-confidence, assurance and strength. They have got to learn to be assertive, firm and dynamic. Teachers should give extra encouragement to girls both to believe in their own ability and sense of self-worth. Education should help in training of skills such as overcoming fear of failure, coping with stress, developing resistance to criticism and willingness to take risks.

Curricula and textbooks should be redesigned to include values and process commensurate with the new status of women.

The main values, identified can be:

1. Respect of the roles performed inside and outside the home
2. Home management, a joint responsibility of all members
3. Equal participation in the development of the nation
4. Equal commitment for work at home and outside by both the sexes
5. Decision making process at all levels to be shared by both the sexes
6. Women not to be projected as sex symbols or prosperity symbols
7. No dependance syndrome but women to be self reliant, self-propelled and self-directed
8. Development of vocational skills and competencies for economic independence.

9. No degrading of women in matrimony such as bride price, dowry, sati etc.

Obviously, empowerment of rural women should be the priority area of non-formal, adult and continuing education programmes. Stress on need based functional education and skill development in the practical utility areas would attract enrolment of girls in non-formal education. People in mass media, folk media, functionaries of voluntary agencies, performing artists and creative workers should be sensitised to promote the identified values of empowerment of women.

REFERENCES

1. Ghadially, Rehana (Ed) *Women in Indian Society*, New Delhi. Sage Publication, 1988.
2. Hughes, Mary and Kennedy, Mary, *New Futures: Changing Women's Education*, Routledge and Kegan Paul, 1985.
3. National Perspective Plan for Women (1988-200 A.D.) Report of the Core Group set up by the Department of Women and Child Development, Ministry of Human Resources Development, Government of India, 1988.
4. Pillai, J.K. *Readings in Women's Education*, Kodaikanal, Mother Teresa Women's University, 1988.
5. Slipman, Sue. *Helping Ourselves to Power*, Oxford. Pergamon Press, 1986.
6. *Towards Equality: Report of the Committee on the Status of Women in India,* Government of India, Department of Social Welfare, Ministry of Education and Social Welfare, New Delhi, December 1974.

4

Women's Reservations Bill

As a landmark in parliamentary history of India Women's Reservation Bill was passed in the Rajya Sabha (Upper House) of Parliament with thumping majority in March 2010. Though some parties pretending upholder of cause of down-trodden and excluded sections of society opposed the Bill and made uproar in the house. The Bill is yet to be passed by Lok Sabha and then to be ratified by majority of state legislative assemblies before it become reality.

It is catastrophic that in the name of women all political parties- major or minor- make huge cry in all sense. When the issue of women's reservation in parliament or state legislatures came no unanimity is seen. Though Congress(I) has Sonia Gandhi as party President, BSP has Mayavati as Supremo, TMC has Mamta Banerji, and other Parties have same notable women politicians, Indian Parliament could not get Women's Reservation Bill pass as yet. Jayalalitha, Uma Bharti, Sushma Swaraj, Margaret Alva, Vasundhara Raje, Vrinda Karat, Renuka Choudhuri, and many more names are there. We have Meira Kumar as Speaker of the Lok Sabha. Despite that, the position of women in politics has always been marginal. Although women constitute half of the world's population, their participation in political life has been negligible all along. Today, at the world level only 10 per cent of parliamentary positions and six per cent of Cabinet ministerial posts are occupied by women.

Only a few countries have crossed 30 per cent representation of women in their Parliament. The position of Indian women in the Parliament has always remained at a very low level never going beyond 10 per cent at any point of time which is very surprising because while societies, which have lesser tradition of public acceptance of women's political participation have witnessed a steady increase in their participation, India's history has taken a backward turn. The sentiment in favour of women being active in politics is nothing new. Women's right to equal political participation including their right to vote was accepted very leniently in India much earlier than most Western societies conceded to this demand. Unlike the West, where the suffragettes had to fight a prolonged battle for right to vote, political rights came to Indian women with relative ease owing to their noticeable participation in the national movement to demand these rights from our colonial rulers.

Even though women in India had benefited from the environment provided by the freedom struggle, and the decolonisation experience, yet, after Independence the movement lost steam. Nothing epitomises the political status of women in India more than the fact that at the threshold of the 21st century they have to demand 33 per cent reservation in Parliament and State Assemblies because they are getting nowhere in the normal course. The track record of women candidates in the last twelve Lok Sabha elections speaks for itself. When India became a sovereign republic, the first Lok Sabha had only 22 women though there was no dearth of suitable candidates at that time.

The second Lok Sabha had 27 women (5.4%), in the third Lok Sabha this improved marginally to 34 (6.7%), whereas the fourth one saw a slump with only 31 women (5.9%). There was a sharp decline when Indira Gandhi was at the peak of her career and only 22 (4.29%) women were elected to the fifth Lok Sabha. The Janata Party came to power in 1977 and there was a further decline in the sixth Lok Sabha (with 3.4%). There was a small increase in 1980 in the seventh Lok Sabha with their figures going up to 28 (5.1%). With the advent of Rajiv Gandhi in 1984, the situation improved somewhat and the figure went up to 44 (8.11%) the highest so far. This declined in the ninth Lok Sabha to 28 (5.29%) when the Janata Dal formed the Government. It went up a little in the tenth Lok Sabha in 1991 and stood at 39 (7.2%). In the eleventh Lok Sabha, it was again 39 women (7.2%). The number has been declining since.

And political parties remain reluctant to field female candidates for election unless they are judged potential winners. Today, women are creating waves and making forays into every male bastion. They have entered the corporate world and have gone into space; they are pilots, soldiers, lawyers and journalists.

There is only one area where their participation has dwindled and that is in the country's political life. Moreover, the agenda of women's empowerment seems to have lost the kind of moral and political legitimacy it enjoyed during the freedom movement, as was evident from the ugly scenes in the aftermath of tabling the Women's Reservation Bill (WRB) in the Parliament in December 1999. Rarely had we faced such a paradoxical situation. On paper (literally) the pre-election manifestos of every major political party—the Congress (I), the BJP, the CPI (M) and the Trinamul Congress had promises to reserve one-third of seats for women in the Lok Sabha and State Legislatures by a Constitutional Amendment. And yet when the Women's Reservation Bill was being sought to be tabled in the Parliament, we witnessed unruly politicians ruggedly tearing it, and shouting it down. After two rounds of raucous rejection first in 1996 under the Deve Gowda government and then in 1998 under the (first) Vajpayee government, the Union Law Minister in December, 1999 managed to introduce the historic as still a part of history, 85th Constitutional Amendment Bill seeking to reserve 33 per cent seats for women in legislative bodies. The bill awaits consideration and debate in the Parliament.

Main Provisions of the Bill

The 85th Constitutional Amendment Bill, 1999, or the Women's Reservation Bill is reproduced below. The Constitutions 85th Amendment Bill, 1999.

Statement of Objects and Reasons

1. Articles 243D and 243T inserted by the Constitution (73rd Amendment) Act, 1992 and the Constitution (74th Amendment) Act, 1992 respectively provide that not less than one-third of the seats shall be reserved for women in every panchayat and every municipality. Further, the said articles provide that, from amongst the seats reserved for the Scheduled Castes (SCs) and the Scheduled Tribes (STs), not less than one-third seats shall be reserved for women belonging to the SCs or, as the case may be, the STs. The said articles also provide that such seats reserved for women may be allotted by rotation to different constituencies.
2. Having provided reservation for women in panchayats and municipalities, it was felt that

reservation for women on the same lines be provided in the House of the People (Lok Sabha) and in the Legislative Assemblies of the states by amending the Constitution. Accordingly, the Constitution (81st Amendment) Bill, 1996 was introduced in the Lok Sabha on 12th September 1996. The said Bill sought to reserve not less than one-third of the total number of seats filled by direct elections in the House of the People and in the Legislative Assemblies of the state; for women, provided the number of seats of the state in the House of the People was more than two.

3. The Bill seeks to achieve the aforesaid objects.

S.2. In Article 239 AA of the Constitution in clause (2), in sub-clause (b), for the words "the SCs and the Women" shall be substituted.

3. After Article 330 of the Constitution, the following article shall be inserted, namely:

330A. (1) Seats shall be reserved for women in the House of the People.

(2) As nearly as may be, one-third of the total number of seats reserved under clause (2) of Article 330 shall be reserved for women belonging to the SCs or the STs, as the case may be:

Provided that where the seat reserved for the SCs or the STs, as the case may be, in relation to a state or Union territory is one, then, in every block comprising of three general elections to the House of the People, the seat in the first general election shall be reserved for women belonging to the SCs or the STs and no seat shall be reserved in the other two general elections:

Provided further that where the seats reserved for the SCs or the STs, as the case may be, in relation to a state or Union Territory are two, then in every block comprising of three general elections to the House of the People.

(a) one seat shall be reserved for women belonging to the SCs or the STs in the first two general elections in such a manner that the same constituency is not reserved for women in both the aforesaid elections; and

(b) no seat shall be reserved for women belonging to the SCs or the STs in the third general election.

(1) As nearly as may be, one-third (including the number of seats reserved for women belonging to the SCs and the STs) of the total numbers of seats to be filled by direct election to the House of the People in a State or Union territory shall be reserved for women and such seats may be allotted by rotation to different constituencies in that State or Union Territory:

Provided that where the seat, not being a seat reserved for the SCs or the STs, in relation to a State or Union territory is one, then, in every block comprising of three general elections to the House of the People, the seat in the first general election shall be reserved for women and no seat shall be so reserved for woken in the other two general elections:

Provided further that where the seats, not being seats reserved for the SCs or the STs, in relation to a state or Union Territory are two, then, in every block comprising of three general elections to the House of the People:

(a) one seat shall be reserved for women in the first two general elections in such a manner that the same constituency is not reserved for women in both the aforesaid elections; and

(b) no seat shall be reserved for women in the third general election.

4. In Article 331 of the Constitution, the following proviso shall be inserted at the end, namely:

"Provided that where such nominations are made in relation to every block comprising of three general elections to the House, one seat shall be reserved for the women of Anglo-Indian community to every House constituted after first two general elections and no seat shall be reserved for the women of that community in the House constituted after the third general election."

5. After Article 332 of the Constitution, the following article shall be inserted, namely:

332A. (1) Seats shall be reserved for women in the Legislative Assembly of every State,

(2) As nearly as may be, one-third of the total number of seats reserved under clause (3) of Article 332 shall be reserved for women belonging to the SCs or the STs, as the case may be:

Provided that where the seat reserved for the SCs or the STs, as the case may be, in relation to a State is one, then, in every block comprising of three general elections to the Legislative Assembly of the State, the seat in the first general election shall be reserved for women belonging to the SCs or the STs, as the case may be:

Provided further that where the seats reserved for the SCs or the STs, as the case may be, in relation to a State are two, then, in every block comprising of three general elections to the Legislative Assembly of that State -

(a) one seat shall be reserved for women belonging to the SCs or the STs in the first two general elections in such a manner that the constituency is not reserved for women in both the aforesaid elections; and

(b) no seat shall be reserved for women belonging to the SCs or the STs in the third general election.

(1) As nearly as may be, one-third (including the number of seats reserved for women belonging to the SCs or the STs) of the total number of seats to be filled by direct election in the Legislative Assembly of every state shall be reserved for women and such seats may be allotted by rotation to different constituencies in that state.

6. In Article 333 of the Constitution, the following proviso shall be inserted at the end, namely:

Provided that where such nomination is made in relation to every block comprising of three general elections to the Assembly, the seat in the Assembly constituted after the first general election shall be reserved for nomination of a woman of the Anglo-

Indian Community and no seat shall be reserved for the women of that community in the Assembly constituted after the second and the third general elections.

7. After Article 334 of the Constitution, the following article shall be inserted namely:

   334 A. Notwithstanding anything in the foregoing provisions of this Part or Part VIII, the provisions of this Constitution relating to the reservation of seats for women in the House of People, the Legislative Assembly of a State and Legislative Assembly of the National Capital Territory of Delhi shall cease to have effect on the expiration of a period of 15 years from the commencement of the Constitution (84lh Amendment) Act, 1998:

   Provided that nothing in this article shall affect any representation in the House of the People, the Legislative Assembly of State or the Legislative Assembly of the National Capital Territory of Delhi until the dissolution of then existing House, Legislative Assembly of a State or the Legislative Assembly of the National Capital Territory of Delhi, as the case may be.

8. The amendments made to the Constitution, by this Act, shall not affect any representation in the House of the People, the Legislative Assembly of a State or the Legislative Assembly of the National Capital Territory of Delhi until the dissolution of the House, the Legislative Assembly of a State or the Legislative Assembly of the National Capital Territory of Delhi, as the case may be, in existence at the commencement of this Act.

On a plain reading of the bill its key provisions emerge as:

1. One-third of all seats in the Lok Sabha and State Legislatives shall be reserved for women.
2. These reservations are for an indefinite period, unlike reservations for SCs and STs which lapse unless extended after every ten years.
3. The reserved constituencies are to be determined through a draw of lots. For SCs and STs, constituencies are reserved on the basis of population proportion. Constituencies with a high SC/ST population are selected for a period of time and are supposed to be delimited after some years. But since the population of women is evenly spread throughout the country, this formula cannot be applied for them. The draw of lots system will mean every time a new set of constituencies will be declared as reserved for women.
4. There is also a provision for parallel reservation for SCs and STs, which is to say women belonging to SCs and STs will be getting one-third of seats reserved for people of that category, *i.e.,* reservations within reservations.

An Assessment

It is pertinent to note that there are many aspects surrounding the history and nature of this Bill and its fallout twice upon being tabled in the Parliament. Instead of creating stiff opposition to the move, what was expected from our Parliamentarians was a reasoned and empirically grounded debate on the reservation package— the extent, location, under what conditions, for what period of time and so on. Their repeated rejection of the Bill showed their self-serving instincts—a case of over 180 MPs in the Lok Sabha facing the prospects of permanently losing their seats to women. (*Seminar,* 457, Sept, 1997, p. 12)

Political leaders and groups have opposed the Bill on grounds like reservations are unconstitutional, undemocratic, elitist, infirm and so on. Rarely is it appreciated that reservations are not a matter of principle, that they are at best a limited intervention in a larger repertoire of affirmative action designed to correct prior distortions. But then, social trends all over the country indicate the anxiety of Central and state governments to embark on a policy of reservation for using classes of people as vote-banks and potential constituencies.

The irony is that such governments instinctively know that the power structure, which has put them where they are, will not tolerate them if they try and change its rules, which makes up for the reason that no party or politician likes to be seen opposing measures that claim to work for women's empowerment but they will fight to keep it out anyway because it is against their interests.

This explains why the very parties that supported the Women's Reservation Bill in their pre-election manifestoes sought to reject it everytime it was tabled in the Parliament. Reservation for women till date remains a volatile and live issue. From the early 90s which witnessed constitutional reservation of seats for women in local government, political empowerment has emerged as a salient issue for the women's movement in India. By far the most significant institutional mechanism to enable women's political participation is reservation for women in local self-government bodies.

Constitutional Amendments in 1992 (mandating a 33

per cent reservation for women in rural panchayats) and 1993 (mandating a 33 per cent reservation for women in urban local governance bodies, such as municipalities) brought large numbers of women into the system. Women's groups argue that reservation for women in the Lok Sabha and the state Assemblies is a natural corollary to their reservation in panchayats and municipalities. (Rashtra Mahila, Vol. 3 , Oct. 1999, p. 2) Somewhat like the Mandal debate the public discussion on the issue has a binary pro and antiquality.

Objections Against the Bill

1. Unconstitutionality of Reservation

Arguments against reservations deny the need for re-distributive justice and affirmative action based on gender. Harping on Article 15 which categorically prohibits discrimination on grounds of religion, sex, caste, birth and a host of other factors —

Article 15(1): The State shall not discriminate against any citizen on grounds only of religion, caste, sex, place of birth or any other reason.

But Article 15(3) is vital since it encapsulates a specific constitutional derogation and dilution from the principle of equality by declaring, "Nothing in this article shall prevent the State from making any special provision for women and children."

Here, then, is the specific constitutional mandate for reverse discrimination on the grounds of sex tailored and focused for the benefit of women of our society. Following upon Article 15, comes Article 16 of the Indian Constitution which focuses exclusively on the specific subject of equality in public/state employment. While Article 16(1) seeks to guarantee equality of opportunity in such employment, Article 16(2) prohibits discrimination in public employment on grounds *inter alia,* of religion, race or sex. Article 16(4) specifically empower' the state to make special provision for backward classes and it was this sub-clause which was held to provide the mandate for the Mandal reservation for OBCs. Consequently, both at the general level of equality and in the specific categories of women, children, backward classes and SC and ST, reservations, special provision and other special schemes have never *per se* been held to be constitutional anathema, but have instead been recognised by specific constitutional provisions like Articles 15(3), 16(4) and 330. *(Seminar,)*

The question which arose in *Andhra Pradesh* v. *Vijay Kumar*, (1994 IV SCC 520) was whether sex based reservation in public employment was constitutionally valid. A particular rule of public employment in the State of Andhra Pradesh which provided, *inter alia,* that other things being equal, women would be given preference for certain categories of public employment, was assailed as being constitutionally invalid. The Supreme Court negated the challenge and upheld the constitutional validity of the legislation in question, principally by reference to the reliance upon Article 15(3) of the Indian Constitution. The Court noted the constitutional schemes of Articles 14 to 16 and held, firstly, that Article 14 and Article 15(1) are the genus whereas Article 15(3), Article 16(1) and Article 16(4) are sub-categories of that genus. The Court further held that Article 15(3) specifically permits special provisions for women and children and Article 15(3) would thus cover and subsume the smaller universe of public employment dealt with in Article 16 and its various sub-clauses. In other words, Article 15(3) would permit discrimination in favour of women and children in all kinds of activities and areas of which public employment dealt with in Article 16 is only a part. Decisions like *Andhra Pradesh* v. *Vijay Kumar* (supra) reinforce the constitutional basis for sex based reservation in our constitutional jurisprudence. An attempt like the proposed Women's Reservation Bill (which is a proposed constitutional amendment Bill), even if statutory in nature, cannot *per se* be said to be vitiated by the vice of unconstitutionality on the ground that our Constitution neither recognises nor permits sex based reservation.

As such the proposed Bill is a constitutional (and not a statutory) amendment Bill and it precludes all arguments of constitutional invalidity save and except the basic structure argument since a constitutional amendment can be challenged only on the grounds of basic structure. It is now well established in our jurisprudence, especially since the landmark judgements of the Supreme Court in *Keshvanand Bharti* (AIR 1973 SC 1461), *Minerva Mills* and *Woman Rao* (1981 2 SCC 362) that the basic structure doctrine frowns only upon alteration of basic features of our Constitution, as for example, conversion of a republic into a monarchy; modification of a democracy into a theocracy, and an abandonment of principles of secularism. Although the basic structure of the Indian Constitution has never (and for obvious reasons, deliberately never) been defined, it clearly involves a *fundamental* abrogation of certain principles governing the Indian polity.

In the very nature of things, the proposed provision of reservation for women in legislatures cannot be said to trench upon any of those fundamental principles of the Indian polity. In any event, it would be anomalous, to say the least, if a dispensation affirmatively recognised and mandated by Article 15(3) of the Constitution can be said to be destructive of the basic structure of the Constitution.

2. *Elitism*

Whereas most politicians pay lip service to the need for reservations of seats for women in Parliament when it has come to actual implementation of the proposed Bill for women's reservation there has been much double speak. The most acrimonious of protest have come from the OBC faction of the Parliament who claim that only the "creamy layer" of upper caste women will benefit from reservation for women.

Their vociferous demand of "sub reservations" for OBCs and minorities within the women's reservation quota has to be viewed in this context. They argue that like the proposed quota within quota in Lok Sabha and Legislative Assemblies for women belonging to the SCs and STs, the Reservation Bill must include a similar quota for OBC women also. The Constitution, under Articles 330 and 332 provides for reservation for SCs and STs in Lok Sabha and Legislative Assemblies in proportion of their population, which at the all-India level works out to about 15 per cent for SCs and seven per cent for STs. Reservation for SCs and STs in representative institutes is thus a constitutional provision and valid. Article 15(4) also allows the state to make special provisions for the advancement of SCs and STs. There is thus, no impediment for providing reservation for women within the reservation for SCs and STs. On the other hand, like for SCs and STs, there is no constitutional reservation for OBCs in Lok Sabha or Legislative Assemblies.

Though after the Mandal Commission Report, reservation has been extended to OBCs, this is only in respect of employment and admission to educational institutions and not in respect of representative institutions. When there is no separate reservation for OBCs in

Parliament and Legislative Houses, can such reservation be provided only in respect of women OBCs?

Ordinarily, reservations violate the principle of equality and are not to be permitted. For providing reservations, some constitutional avenue must be open. What is the Constitutional basis of reservation for OBCs?

Article 15(4) provides:

> Nothing in this Article... shall prevent the State from making any special provision for the advancement of any socially or educationally backward classes of citizens or for the Scheduled Castes and Scheduled Tribes.

It was to determine the 'socially or educationally backward classes of citizens' that the Mandal Commission was constituted and the Commission gave a list of castes and sub-castes which are known as the OBCs (Other Backward Classes). The Supreme Court, in the Mandal Commission Judgement has approved reservation for OBCs as permissible under Article 15(4).

Though the Supreme Court was dealing with reservation in educational institutions and in employment, the fact of the matter is that the Court has accepted the Mandal list as the valid list of OBCs and has also accepted the proposition that the phrase 'special provisions' in Article 15(4) would include reservation for OBCs.

It is therefore possible to argue that reservation for OBCs even in Parliament and Assemblies is permissible. Adequacy of representation is the criteria for deciding reservation in government jobs but not necessarily for other reservations.

Article 16 of the Constitution deals with equality in public employment. Article 16(4) which is concerned with reservation in public employment reads:

> Nothing in this article shall prevent the State from making any provision for the reservation of appointments or posts in favour of any backward class of citizens which, in the opinion of the State, is not adequately represented in the services under the State.

Notably, for other types of reservation, such as reservation in educational institutions or reservations in representative institutions, such a criteria, *i.e.,* of adequacy of representation does not exist.

It can still be argued that in any event, the whole purpose of all kinds of reservation is to ensure adequate representation and any reservation would have to meet this test. Even so, an isolated instance of break-up of MPs in a particular Lok Sabha cannot be the sole test of determining the necessity of reservation. One has to see the representation of OBC MLAs in Legislative Assemblies and in earlier Lok Sabhas to see whether the present situation is an isolated instance or a consistent trend.

The purpose of reservation is no doubt to provide adequate representation, not just once or twice but consistently and over a period so that representation of that group becomes a regular reality. But even if reservations for OBCs generally may be a debatable proposition, reservation for women OBCs is on a much factual and empirical footing. Even though there are more than 200 OBC MPs in the present Lok Sabha, very few of them are women. Same is the case in Assemblies and even historically in the past.

As such a combination of two factors, namely inadequate representation of women OBCs in representative institutions coupled with the fact that OBCs have been constitutionally recognised as educationally and socially backward suggests a strong case for reservation for women belonging to OBC.

It is important to note that it is the combined effect of both the factors that leads to a strong argument for reservation for OBC women.

If mere inadequate representation was a sufficient criteria for reservation it would also entitle Brahmin and Rajput women for quotas within quota. It is the further fact of educational and social backwardness which leads to the necessity of separate reservation.

This is an extremely crucial argument, even when we discuss reservation for women belonging to religious minorities. Some persons have argued that if there is no reservation for OBCs generally in representative institutions how can there be reservation for OBC women? This argument however does not have much of a legal basis. Reservation is an enabling provision. Despite observations by the Supreme Court from time to time that reservation is not an exception to the rule of equality but is a facet of the fundamental right of equality, no Court has as yet ever directed the government to provide reservations where none exists.

No Court has yet asked any government to include a particular caste or sub-caste in the list of SCs, STs or OBCs if the government has chosen not to include such a caste or sub-caste in the list. The judiciary's decisions over the years clearly reflect the attitude that it is entirely for the government to provide or not to provide reservation and the judiciary comes into the picture only once such reservation is already provided by the government and is challenged as the one breaching fundamental rights.

Thus merely because OBCs are recognised as educationally and socially backward, it is not necessary for the government to provide reservation for them. Even while providing reservation, it is entirely for the government to decide whether to provide such reservation only in employment and admissions or also in representative institutions. Similarly, it is for the government to decide whether to provide reservation in representative institutions for OBCs as a whole or to some section of it, provided that section can be clearly distinguished from the other sections. Women are definitely a clearly classifiable section and thus providing reservation for OBC women without providing a general reservation of OBCs has no legal impediment. A strong argument against such reservation is that, in any case, even without reservation there are more than 200 MPs belonging to the OBC in the Lok Sabha and thus their representation is not inadequate. Besides, the issue was never raised at the time of reservation for women at Panchayat level.

The vociferous demand of the Yadav faction has been made not to ensure OBC women's representation or participation but to maintain or strengthen the OBC numbers in Parliament. Merely because OBCs are recognised as educationally and socially backward, it is not necessary for the government to provide reservation for them. Similarly, those seeking reservation for religious minorities must look at Article 15(1). Special favours on ground of religion are barred. They are also barred on grounds of sex and caste but the same Article 15(3) and (4) protects reservation for women and SCs and STs. No such protective measure exists on grounds of religion or for religious minorities.

Thus, reservation on grounds of religion would be clearly unconstitutional. In the face of such demands of reservations within reservations, we must keep in mind the purpose for demanding reservation in representative bodies. The major function of these bodies is to formulate the laws and policies governing the nation and its various sections. Representation to each section is an impossibility as taking it to its logical absurdity, each of them has more than 4. 000 castes and sub-castes, apart from various other groupings like every dialect, culture and sub-culture would have to be given representation. This is not just chaotic but totally absurd.

3. Undemocratic Nature

Again, those who argue that reservations are undemocratic work on this premise that political participation is a voluntary activity including among the rights to vote, canvass and campaign for elections, a right also to contest an election. If women have made their presence felt in every field they should strive to create a niche for themselves in politics also. These people fail to see the factors that have resulted in the complete marginalisation of women in politics after independence.

Prior to our independence, in the 1930s and 1940s there were more women leaders at all levels in the Congress alone than there are found today in all the parties together. Why were a whole generation of women leaders who were active at the forefront of our freedom struggle denied a substantial presence in Parliament and State Assemblies upon independence specially considering that the social opinion in India has been in favour of their participation.

Upon Independence the women's front of the Congress (the Mahila Congress) began to be systematically sidelined as the party was taken over by power hungry politicians who turned it into an instrument of authoritarian rule. Jawaharlal Nehru, who became the first Prime Minister of India was though committed to social transformation, yet he could not free the machinery of governance from the colonial policy of political subjugation and allowed the bureaucracy to maintain its stranglehold over society. The constructive programmes of the Congress Party that evolved under Gandhi's leadership were transformed into the community development programmes run and controlled by bureaucrats.

Thus the Nehru era set into motion widespread depoliticisation of our society by snatching away all power and initiative from local communities and providing bureaucrats and party politicians with several vicious levers of control and manipulation. The marginalisation of women in political parties was part of this process. Under this system dedicated social workers and elected representatives could survive only if they appeared before the bureaucracy as grovelling supplicants and who entered into a nexus of loot and plunder with them.

In fact, Indira Gandhi started the practice of nominations by the 'High Command' to party posts as well as distribution of party tickets for elections. At the same time the Congress systematically went about subverting fledgling institutions of democracy at various levels. With decision-making bodies getting more and more remote from people's lives due to over centralisation of power, the few women who were active in the party were further marginalised. Getting a party ticket was no longer easy for credible self-respecting women political workers in villages, districts or cities.

It became necessary to be close to power brokers with influence in the Delhi darbar in order to qualify for any post in the party or an opportunity to contest elections which meant seriously jeopardising their reputation. We all agree that most male politicians today insist on personal *haziri* before they decide to give a seat nomination. As a result before each election, one comes across women being pushed from one politician's house to another as they try to get a nomination which keeps them in politics.

The criteria in giving a ticket is always—does she have the funds to fight the elections, is she of a numerically dominant class or caste of particular constituency, will she assert herself? Many potential women aspirants have complained that lack of money, muscle power and the mafia have prevented party men from giving them the tickets.

The factors that inhibit the entry of women into politics go beyond discrimination against them in the distribution of tickets. The regime of restrictions that most women live under, within their families and communities, their load of domestic responsibilities and lack of financial autonomy (given that very few women inherit or own property and most are prevented from even earning an independent livelihood) makes it virtually impossible for them to take an active part in politics even at the neighbourhood level.

Therefore, only those few women who have the backing of their families, especially of prominent male members, can hope to gain a foothold in the political world. Any polity in which violence and crime dominate, women as a group become automatically marginalised—partly out of choice but largely due to the fact that barring exceptions, women cannot effectively compete with men in gangsterism. Sooner or later they lose out and just as well.

4. Futality of Rotation System

The bill provides for reserving particular constituencies for women, i. *e.,* reserving seats exclusively for women through constituencies. This reservation shall be brought about by draw of lots at the time of each election. There is a serious flaw in this provision. The draw of lots system of gender reservation will mean that every time a new set of constituencies will be declared as reserved for women. There would be no way to predict whose turn will come next. In a functioning democracy, politicians are expected to develop and nurse a constituency. The fundamental principle of electoral democracy is a substantial link between the electors and the elected and a continuing element of responsibility towards the electorate.

A change of constituency every five years (and in the contemporary scenario of political instability, possibly more frequently) would snap that fundamental link between the electorate and the elected and will eliminate all incentive and interest in the development of the constituency because in the next election and draw of lots that constituency may go to another candidate.

Such a move jeopardises the possibility of sensible planning to contest and nurture a political constituency for both male and female candidates. It will make them much more dependent upon their parties for winning the next election. As legislators will not have the incentive to seek re-election from the same constituency plunder will increase and politics will be even more predatory and unaccountable. The present scheme of reservations will ensure that women will enter the electoral battle only against other women and never get an opportunity to contest on their own merit on a general seat. This will brand them as 'quota' candidates or light weight politicians. This has happened with SCs and STs who have been permanently ghettoised to reserved constituencies.

5. Question of 33 per cent

The objection of the anti-group to the magic number of 33 per cent reservation is also tenable, 33 per cent is by no means a small figure. If after the SC, ST reservations a further 33 per cent is reserved for women, the general open seats will be reduced to 50 per cent of the total. Even if we presume that the Bill gets passed in the coming session our Parliament would have to accommodate 180 women candidates who may not necessarily have any political experience, who may be semi-literate or unaware completely of the awesome task of policy making at the macro level.

Doling out such a large percentage of seats to such candidates will definitely bring about a further lowering of our Parliament's standard. The Parliament ought to be a forum for the most seasoned, thoughtful and well informed individuals among us, it is no place for political novices to learn their first lessons in parliamentary democracy.

6. Non-uniform Approach

Unlike the 73rd and 74th Amendments which only exempted the three tribal states of Meghalaya, Mizoram and Nagaland the present bill exempts all those states and UTs from where there are less than three members in the Parliament, from adopting reservation for women. By this logic, almost the entire North-east (except Assam), Sikkim, all the Union Territories (except Delhi) will not have any reservation or representation for women. This will mean 171 and not 181 (one-third of 543) women.

One of the suggestions is that these states should be grouped together and women's reservation rotated among them, as in all these years only occasionally a woman has come up from these areas. Again, unlike the 73rd and 74th Amendments which formed a wholistic piece by taking care of the total representation, the 81st Amendment Bill is a piecemeal attempt. The hurried way in which the Bill has been formulated has led to certain doubts about flaws in the Bill.

This has been exploited by the males (including the SC/ST men) to create dilemmas even in the minds of those who had authored the Bill and make them dither from their stand. Certainly, the issues are very complex and highly debatable. No one today seriously contests that five decades of democratic politics and planned interventions through legislation and public programmes for women has not made a serious dent in the status of women. Critics of the existing provisions of reservation in the Constitution as cause of increased hostilities, rivalries and political instability ignore the fact that without the triple provisions for reservation for the depressed classes in education, public employment and political representation, the kind of breaches that have been made in the thousands of year old institutions of 'social exclusion' would not have taken place and India's claim as the world's largest democracy would have remained a misnomer.

What is needed urgently is interventions at the policy level by women themselves. Why is women's participation in policy and decision-making important and how does one go about improving it? This has to be seen in the present context of women's marginalisation through development policies and the ineffectiveness of constitutional and legal provisions for gender equality. The formulation of development policies and special programmes for women have the effect of relegating them to a minority category of beneficiaries and not, actors and decision-makers for their welfare and improvement. Women, who constitute half of the country's population certainly deserve a better deal than spasmodic doles of mercy.

They have to have a say not only in things that concern them directly but in all matters that affect the society in so far as they also have the status of citizens. There are moments in the history of a nation when the same idea grips it at the same time.

Though after an unprecedented roar in parliament, the Women's Reservation Bill 2010 has been passed in Rajya Sabha by a thumping majority, it yet is to be passed by the Lok Sabha which is a difficult task.

Later or sooner we will be able `to repay the debt to our mothers said Veerappa Moily in the Rajya Sabha.

REFERENCES

1. *Indra Sawhney* vs. *Union of India,* AJR 1993 SC 477: (923 SUP- SCC 217).
2. *Kali's Yug-Women and Law Journal,* March 2000, p. 62.
3. Madhu Kishwar, "Taking on the Challenge", *The Hindustan Times,* May 16, 1996.
4. Madhu Kishwar, "Women and Politics: Beyond Quotas", *Economic and Political Weekly,* October 26, 1996, p. 2867.
5. NGO Country Report on Beijing Plus Five — From the Indian Women's Movement, May 8, 2000, p. 36.
6. Pramila Dandvate, "...like a flower pot in a drawing room", *The Times of India,* July 21, 1996.
7. *Rashtra Mahila,* Vol. 3, October 1999, p. 2.
8. Ravinder K. Verma and Gyanender K. Verma, "Women in Bihar Politics", *Economic and Political Weekly,* April 13, 1996, p. 935.
9. *Seminar,* 457, September 1997, p. 12.
10. Shanta Serbjeel Singh, "A Feminine Critique", 1998, p. 22.
11. Sushieela Kaushik, "Why Women in Legislatures", Paper presented at the Meet of Parliamentarians (NCW), November 19, 1996.
12. Usha Narayanan, "Women's Political Empowerment: Imperatives and Challenges", *Mainstream,* April 10, 1999, p. 1.

5

Indian Scenario and Statutory Measures

"It is much more necesary to cure the soul than the body, for death is better than a bad life.

—Epictetus

The women were accorded high status in India since yore days. Religious literature and scripture have ample testimony to this—but from medieval ages onwards their condition deteriorated. Still women are discriminated in all walks of life. Constitutional measures have, no doubt, ascertained some privileges for than. But man-domination is deeply rooted in Indian psyche. In protest to Women's Reservation Bill. SP's supremo Mulayam Singh Yadav's comment of 27th March 2010 is an ample of this.

However in the present chapter we will address women leadership after the 73rd constitutional Amendment in India.

Basically, the necessity of the Constitution (73rd) Amendment Act, 1992 arose in view of the ineffectiveness of the Panchayati Raj Institutions which were in existence for a long time. Necessity, was felt that the PRIs could not gain the status and dignity of viable and responsive peoples' bodies due to absence of regular elections, prolonged supersessions, inadequate representation of weaker sections of society, insufficient delegation of powers, lack of financial resources, etc.

The 73rd Constitutional Amendment has accordingly provided for the constitution and composition of the Panchayats at various levels, reservation of seats for weaker sectionsspecially dalits and women, regular elections, devolution of powers, authority and responsibilities, constitution of Finance Commission to review financial position, regular audit of Panchayats etc.

In fact, the main provisions of the Act can be broadly classified under two heads — (a) the provisions which are mandatory for the States and (b) the areas which have been left for the State legislatures to take decisions keeping in view the socioeconomic conditions and other factors of their State. The mandatory provisions of the Central Act are compulusory to be included in the legislations to be enacted by the States and in case of discretionary features of the Act it would be upto the State to take decisions of their own.

1. MANDATORY PROVISIONS

First, we will highlight the mandatory provisions in broad parlance.

(a) Constitution of Panchayats

The Central Act has prescribed a three-tier system of Panchayats and in each State there shall be Panchayats at the village, intermediate and district levels. However, Panchayats at the intermediate level may not be constituted in a State having a population not exceeding 20 lakh.

(b) Composition of Panchayats

As per provision, all the seats in a Panchayat shall be filled by persons chosen by direct election from territorial constituencies in the Panchayat area and for this purpose, each Panchayat area shall be divided into territorial constituencies in such manner that the ratio between the population of each constituency and the number of seats allotted to it shall, so far as practicable, be the same throughout the Panchayat area. A person who has attained the age of 21 years can contest the election for being chosen as a member of a Panchayat. The validity of any law relating to the delimitation shall not be called in question in any court. Similarly no election to any Panchayat shall be called in question except by an election petition presented to such authority and in such manner as is provided by the legislature of the State.

The superintendence, direction and control of the preparation of electoral rolls and the conduct of all elections to the Panchayats shall be vested in the State Election Commission consisting of a State Election Commissioner to be appointed by the State Government. The chairperson of a Panchayat at the intermediate and district levels shall be elected by and from amongst the elected members thereof and the chairperson and other members of a Panchayat whether or not chosen by direct election from territorial constituencies in the Panchayat area shall have the right to vote in the meetings of the Panchayats.

(c) Reservation of Seats

Seats shall be reserved for (a) the Scheduled Castes, and (b) Scheduled Tribes in every Panchayat and the number of seats so reserved shall bear, as nearly as may be, the same proportion to the total number of seats to be filled by direct election in that Panchayat as the population of the Scheduled Castes in that Panchayat area or of the Scheduled Tribes in that Panchayat area bears to the total population of that area and such seats may be allotted by rotation to different constituencies in a Panchayat.

Not less than one-third of the total number of seats reserved for the Scheduled Castes or the Scheduled Tribes shall be reserved for women belonging to the Scheduled Castes or the Scheduled Tribes as the case may be. Similarly, in case of general seats also one-third of them shall be reserved for women belonging to any class or category and such seats may be allotted by rotation to different constituencies in a Panchayat.

Again, such number of offices of chairpersons at each level shall be reserved for the Scheduled Castes and the Scheduled Tribes that the proportion of the number to be reserved to the total number of such offices in the Panchayat at each level is the same as the population of the Scheduled Castes or of the Scheduled Tribes in the State bears to the total population of the State and not less than one-third of the offices so reserved shall be reserved for women belonging to the concerned category.

Similarly, one-third of the number of offices left for the general category at each level shall be reserved for women belonging to any class or category and all reservations shall be done on rotation basis.

(d) Duration of Panchayats

A Panchayat shall have a term of five years and if it is dissolved earlier for any reason, fresh election shall be held within six months from the date of its dissolution. In case the remainder of the period is less than six months, it shall not be necessary to hold any election for constituting the Panchayat for such period. A Panchayat constituted upon the dissolution of a Panchayat before the expiration of its duration shall continue only for the remainder of the period for which the dissolved Panchayat would have continued had it not been so dissolved.

(e) Constitution of State Finance Commission

The Governor of a State shall constitute a Finance Commission within one year and thereafter at the expiration of every fifth year, to review the financial position of the Panchayats and to make recommendations to the Governor as to:

(a) the principles which should govern:

   (i) the distribution between the State and the Panchayats of the net proceeds of the taxes, duties, tolls and fees leviable by the State which may be divided between them under this part and the allocation between the Panchayats at all levels of their respective shares of such proceeds;

   (ii) the determination of the taxes, duties, tolls and fees which may be assigned to or appropriated by the Panchayats;

   (iii) the grants-in-aid to the Panchayats from the Consolidated Fund of the State;

(b) the measures needed to improve the financial position of the Panchayats;

(c) any other matter referred to the Finance Commission by the Governor in the interest of sound finance of the Panchayats.

Through Constitution (Seventy-Third) Amendment Act, 1992 a sub-clause (b) has been inserted in Article 280 of the Constitution. According to this sub-clause the Central Finance Commission, in addition to other recommendations, shall make recommendations to the President as to the measures needed to augment the Consolidated Fund of a State to supplement the resources of the Panchayats in the State on the basis of the recommendations made by the Finance Commission of the State.

(f) District Planning Committee

The provision for constituting a District Planning Committee was made under the Constitution (Seventy-Fourth) Amendment Act, 1992. According to this Act, there shall be a District Planning Committee at the district level to consolidate the plans prepared by the Panchayats and Municipalities in the district and to prepare a draft development plan for the district as a whole.

2. DISCRETIONARY PROVISIONS

In fact, the subject of Panchayati Raj Institutions comes under the State List in the Indian Federal system. Hence any interference by the Centre relating to these Institutions may be construed as an intrusion in the spheres of the working of the States. The Central Act has, therefore, given adequate discretionary powers on the subjects like composition of the Panchayats, devolution of powers to them, their financial matters etc. Under the Central Act the following areas have been left to State legislatures to make suitable provisions in their Acts on the subject keeping in view the overall objects as laid down in the Constitutional Amendment Act.

1. Nomenclature of the Panchayats at different levels.
2. Nomenclature of the chairpersons of Panchayats at various levels.

3. Size in terms of population and area for determination of Panchayats at the village and intermediate levels.
4. Powers and functions of the Gram Sabha.
5. Composition of the Panchayats at different levels: Provided that the ratio between the population of the territorial area of a Panchayat at any level and the number of seats in such Panchayat to be filled by election shall, so far as practicable, be the same throughout the State.
6. To provide or not for the representation of:
   (a) the chairpersons of the Village Panchayats in the Panchayat at the intermediate level and of the chairpersons of the Panchayats at the intermediate level in the Panchayats at the district level;
   (b) the members of the House of People and the members of the Legislative Assembly of the State represeting constituencies which comprise wholly or partly a Panchayat area at a level other than the village level in such Panchayat;
   (c) the members of the Council of States and the members of the Legislative Council of the State where they are registered as electors.
7. The mode of election of the chairperson of a Panchayat at the village level.
8. The manner in which the seats of the members of the Panchayats at different levels shall be reserved for the Scheduled Castes, the Scheduled Tribes and women. Provided that the number of seats reserved

shall be allotted by rotation to different territorial constituencies at each level.

9. The manner in which the offices of the chairpersons at different levels shall be reserved for the Scheduled Castes, the Scheduled Tribes and women. Provided that the number of offices reserved shall be allotted by rotation to different Panchayats at each level.

10. To provide or not for reservation of seats in any Panchayat or offices of chairpersons in the Panchayats at any level in favour of backward class of citizens.

11. To endow the Panchayats at various levels with such powers and authority as may be necessary to enable them to function as institutions of self-government and to make provisions for the devolution of powers and responsibilities upon Panchayats at the appropriate level with respect to:
    (a) the preparation of plans for economic development and social justice;
    (b) the implementation of schemes for economic development and social justice entrusted to them including those relation to the matters listed in the Eleventh schedule of the Constitution.

12. To decide the taxes, ailes, toils and fees for which a Panchayat shall be authorised and also to lay down the procedure and limits for the same.

13. To decide the limits and the conditions of the taxes, duties, tolls and fees which shall be Saved and collected by the State Government but shall be assigned to the Panchayats.

14. To decide the amount or grants-in-aid which shall be provided to the Panchayats from the Consolidated Fund of the State.

15. To authorise the Panchayats at different levels to create a Fund for crediting; all money received, respectively, by or on behalf of the Panchayats and also for the withdrawal of such money thereform.

16. To provide for the composition of the Finance Commission, the qualifications which shall be requisite for appointment as members thereof and the manner in which they shall be selected. The Commission shall determine their procedure and shall have such powers in the performance of their functions as the Legislature of the state, by law, confer on them. The Governor shall cause every recommendation made by the Commission under this article together with an explanatory memorandum as to the action taken thereon to be laid before the Legislature of the State.

17. To make provisions with respect to the maintenance of accounts by Panchayats and the auditing of such accounts.

18. To determine the conditions of service and tenure of office of the State Election Commissioner and to make provision with respect to all matters relating to or in connection with election to the Panchayats.

Provided that the State Election Commissioner shall not be removed from his office except in like manner and on the like grounds as a judge of a High Court. The conditions of service of the State Election Commissioner shall not be varied to his disadvantage after his appointment. The Governor of the State, when so required by the State

Election Commission, make available such staff as may be necessary for the discharge of the functions conferred on the Commission.

19. To make provision with respect to all matters relating to, or in connection with, elections to the Panchayats.

20. To make provisions with respect to:

    (a) the composition and functions of the District Planning Committee;

    (b) the manner in which the chairperson of the District Planning Committee shall be filled: provided that not less than four-fifths of the total number of members of the committee shall be elected by and from amongst, the elected members of the Panchayat at the district level and of the Municipalities in the district in proportion to the ratio between the population of rural areas and of the urban areas in the district.

21. Any provision or any law relating to Panchayats in force in a State immediately before the commencement of the Constitution (Seventy-Third) Amendment Act, 1992, which is consistent with the provisions of this Part," shall continue to be inforce until amended or repealed by a competent Legislature or other competent Authority or until the expiration of one year from such commencement, whichever is earlier : Provided that all the Panchayats existing immediately before such commencement shall continue till the expiration of their duration, unless sooner dissolved by a resolution passed, to that effect by the Legislative Assembly of that State, or in the case of a State having a Legislative Council, by each House of the Legislature of that State.

Thus, it becomes obvious from the discussion that Constitution (73rd) Amendment Act is a land-mark in the direction of empowering women, particularly rural women.

In the next chapter will discuss the womenpower and women leadership in the post-amendment era.

6

Womenpower After Constitution (73rd) Amendment

> "The future of society is in the hand of mothers: if the world was lost through woman, she alone can save it."
>
> —*Louis de Beaufort*

Though as a now (2010) we have ample constitutional support for boosting womenpower, still due to indifference of law-enforcing machinery our womenpower is not fully in a position of benefit.

Here in this chapter we assess the position in the Post-Seventy-Third Constitutional Amendment era.

Remarkably, with the enactment of the Constitution (Seventy-Third) Amendment Act, 1992, on 24 April, 1993, the State Legislatures were required to amend their relevant Acts and Laws or bring out a new Act or Acts replacing the ties Acts within one year. Accordingly, all the States have made the necessary provisions in order to satisfy the requirements of the Constitutional Amendment. The States of Uttar Pradesh, Maharashtra, West Bengal and Orissa have made necessary amendments in their existing Acts, whereas, the rest of the States have replaced the old Acts by new Acts for the purpose. It is notable that in Orissa there is a separate Act for each tier of Panchayati Raj and in Uttar Pradesh and Maharashtra there are two separate Acts, one governing the Panchayats at the village level and the other for the Panchayats at the intermediate and district levels. In other States there is a unified Act governing all the three tiers.

It is interesting to observe that prior to Constitutional Amendment in most of the States there were two separate Acts governing the Panchayati Raj bodies in the State and Orissa had as many as three separate Acts. However, the States of Gujarat, Himachal Pradesh and West Bengal had a single Act each for controlling the activities of the Panchayati Raj Institutions in the State. As regards the mandatory clauses of the Amendment Act, there was no option for the State Legislatures but to incorporate the same in their relevant Acts. However, in case of areas left for the States, there is, naturally, some variation from State to State. For the purposes of analysis such areas have been categorised under the following seven heads.

I. Structure

(i) Three-Tier System

Basically, the 73rd Constitution Amendment has prescribed a three-tier system of Panchayati Raj (or all such States which have population over 20 lakhs. Accordingly, all the 16 major States of the country under study have adopted a three-tier system, the first at the village or group of villages level (lowest level), the second at the block, (intermediate) level and the third at the district (upper) level. Earlier Kerala and Haryana had a two-tier arrangement. Haryana did not have the district level and Kerala the intermediate level tiers.

(ii) Gram Sabha

Gram Sabha has been viewed as roots of democracy and an effective tool for the participation and involvement of the people in the democratic process. Diwakar Committee (1963) emphasised that the Gram Sabha could alone help to create a climate which would secure the essentials of democracy and endow the total governmental structure of the village community with a social base. Gram Sabha refers to a body consisting of all members of the village/ group of villages whose names are registered in the electoral rolls of the Gram Panchayat. In most of the States village means any local area, recorded as a village in the revenue records of the district in which it is situated.

According to Seventy-Third Constitution Amendment Act, 1992, 'village' means a village specified by the Governor by public notification to be a village and includes a group of villages so specified. Similarly, a Gram Sabha has been defined as a body consisting of persons registered in the rolls relating to a village comprised within the area of Panchayat at the village level. A Gram Sabha may exercise such powers and perform such functions at the village level as the Legislature of a State may by law provide.

Prior to the Constitutional Amendment Gram Sabha existed in all the States and in most of the States the Gram Sabha used to be a body corporate having perpetual succession and a common seal and vested with the capacity of suing or being sued in Its corporate name, of acquiring, holding or tranferring property and of entering into contracts. After the Amendment except for Orissa this position of the Gram Sabha has been taken over by the Gram Panchayat which in many States used to be the Executive Committee of the Gram Sabha.

However, at present also a Gram Sabha has to perform very important functions. A Gram Sabha is required to meet from time to time and give its recommendations and suggestions to the Gram Panchayat for its due consideration The meetings of the Gram Sabha shall be presided-over by the chairperson of the Gram Panchayat. In most of the States the major functions of the Gram Sabha include to have discussions and make recommendations and suggestions on the annual statement of accounts, audit notes and annual administration report in respect of development programmes of the Gram Panchayat.

In some States promotion of unity and harmony among all sections of the society in the village, mobilising voluntary labour and contributions in kind and cash for the community welfare programmes, identification of beneficiaries for the implementation of development schemes pertaining to the village and promoting the programme of adult education in the village are also the functions of the Gram Sabha.

(iii) Nomenclature of the Panchayat and the Chairpersons

As is observed there is no uniformity in the nomenclatures used in different States for the Panchayats and chairpersons at different levels. Out of the 16 major States of the country under study most of the States have used the word 'Gram Panchayat' for the Panchayat at the village level. However, four States (Gujarat, Kerala, Maharashtra and Tamil Nadu) have used the nomenclature 'Village Panchayat'. In case of the Panchayat at the intermediate level, eight nomenclatures have been used. Eight States have used the word 'Panchayat Samiti', two States (Gujarat, and Karnataka) as 'Taluka Panchayat' and the remaining six States have used different nomenclatures like Mandal Parishad in Andhra Pradesh, Anchalik Panchayat in Assam Block Panchayat in Kerala, Janpad Panchayat in Madhya Pradesh, Panchayat Union Council in Tamil Nadu and Kshettra Panchayat in Uttar Pradesh.

At the district level, only three nomenclatures have been used. Ten States have used the word 'Zilla Parishad' and three States (Gujarat, Kerala and Tamil Nadu) as 'District Panchayat and the rest of the three States (Madhya Pradesh, Maharashtra and Uttar Pradesh) have used the word 'Zilla Panchayat'.

Coming to the office bearers, in case of chairperson of the Panchayat at the village level eight States have used the word 'Sarpanch', three States (Himachal Pradesh. Uttar Pradesh and West Bengal) as Pradhan and, three States (Assam, Kerala and Tamil nadu) as President. The chairperson of the village level Panchayat is designated as Mukhya in Bihar and Adhyaksha in Karnataka. Similarly six nomenclatures have been used for the chairperson at the intermediate level. Five States have used the were 'President', another six as 'chairman', two (Bihar and Uttar Pradesh) as Pramukh. The chairperson is known as Adhyaksh in Karnataka, Pradhan in Rajasthan and Sabhapati in West Bengal. At the district level also five nomenclatures hove been used. Eight States have used the word 'President' four States as 'Chairman', two States (Karnataka and Uttar Pradesh) as 'Adhyaksha'. The chairperson is known as 'Pramukh' in Rajasthan and 'Sabhadhipati' in West Bengal.

It is interesting to note that while Uttar Pradesh has used the word 'Pramukh' for the chairperson of the Panchayat at the intermediate level, Rajasthan has used the same word for the chairperson at the district level. Some of the States have used the same nomenclature like 'chairman' or Adhyaksha for the chairpersons at both the levels i.e. the intermediate and the district levels. It appears that there is not much change in the nomenclatures used by various States now from the nomenclatures used earlier and only minor changes have been made in case of some other States. For example in Uttar Pradesh the word 'Kshettra Samiti' has been replaced by the nomenclature 'Kshettra Panchayat' and Zilla Parishad by Zilla Panchayat.

As Already mentioned it is also apparent that there is no uniformity in the nomenclatures used by different States. For illustration in. Uttar Pradesh the word 'Pramukh' has been used for the chairperson at the intermediate level, whereas, in the case of Rajasthan it has been for the chairperson at the district level, there are many other examples of the type. In Karnataka the word 'Adhyaksha' and in Assam the word 'President' have been used for the chairpersons at all the three tiers.

(iv) Size of a Panchayat at the Village Level

Notably, there are considerable variations in deciding the minimum size for constituting a Panchayat at the village level, notable that most of the States have not adopted the criterion of viability inspite of the fact that the bigger Gram panchayats have shown better results in terms of financial feasibility of projects, etc. Most of the States did not disturb the earlier arrangement and have constituted a separate Panchayat for each village irrespective of its size.

However, there are two States (Bihar and Karnataka) which have kept in view the concept of viability, Bihar has fixed a minimum size of 7,000 population of the village (s) for constituting a Village Panchayat and Karnataka has fixed 5,000 for the purpose.

Orissa comes next which has prescribed a minimum population of 2,000 for the purpose. Uttar Pradesh, Himachal Pradesh and Assam have fixed a minimum size of 1,000, Tamil Nadu 500 and Punjab 200 for constituting a Panchayat at the village level. There is no doubt that it was a difficult exercise to disturb the old pattern and adopt the criteria of viability under which a number of village Panchayats had to lose their separate identity. This decision might have serious political repurcussions which most of the States wanted to avoid.

Prior to 73rd Amendment the average population per Gram Panchayat was as follows : Kerala (20,512), West Bengal (11,945), Karnataka (10,081), Assam (7,000), Orissa (5,343). Bihar (5,251), Tamil Nadu (3,837), Rajasthan (3,680), Madhya Pradesh (3,000). Andhra Pradesh (2,108). Gujarat (1,764). Haryana (1,744). Maharashtra (1,653), Himachal Pradesh (1,639), Uttar Pradesh (1,230) and Punjab (1,108). It is notable that the average size of population of a Gram Panchayat in Kerala was about 17 times that of a Gram Panchayat in Uttar Pradesh. As regards the average number of villages per Gram Panchayat there were ten or more villages per Gram Panchayat in West Bengal (11.5), Orissa (11.5), Karnataka (10.7) and Assam (10). However, half of the States had less than two villages per Gram Panchayat.

(v) Membership Size for the Panchayat at the Village Level

Under the Constitutional Amendment it has been provided that there shall be direct election for the members of the Panchayats at all levels on the basis of territorial constituencies in such a manner that the ratio between the population of each constituency and the number of seats allotted to it shall, as far as practicable, be the same throughout the Panchayat area.

It is notable that except for Punjab all the States have opted for a single member constituency.

In Punjab each Gram Sabha shall be treated to be a multi-member single constituency and the number of members to be elected shall be determined according to the size of the Gram Sabha, the number varying between 5 and 13.

As regards the size of membership in different Panchayats a number of patterns have been adopted. Some of the States have fixed the minimum and maximum number of members to be elected keeping in view the size of population of concerned Panchayat area. On the other hand in some States population norms in terms of per member have been prescribed. There are some States where ranges have been prescribed. In case of Gujarat there shall be seven members in a Gram Panchayat area upto a population of three thousand and for every additional one thousand population two- members.

In case of Assam the number of members to be elected has been fixed at ten irrespective of the size of the Gram Panchayat area, in Rajasthan there shall be at least five members and no maximum limit has been fixed.

The range from minimum to maximum number of members to be elected in different States also varies from State to State. In case of U.P. the number varies between 9 and 15 against West Bengal between 5 and 30.

(vi) Mode of Election for the Chairperson of the Panchayat at the Village Level

Regarding the mode of election for the chairperson of the Panchayats at the intermediate and district levels there was no option as under the Constitutional Amendment there is a provision for indirect election alone. The chairperson shall be elected by the directly elected members of the Panchayats at the respective levels and it was only at the village Panchayat level that the State Legislatures were left free to decide about the mode of election.

In this regard there were two options: (a) a direct election method under which all the registered voters in the Gram Panchayat area shall elect the chairperson and (b) an indirect election method under which only the directly elected members of the Gram Panchayat shall elect the chairperson.

It is notable that most of States have opted for the direct election method. However, the States of Karnataka, Kerala, Maharashtra and West Bengal have opted for the indirect method of election.

(vii) Reservation for Backward Classes in Panchayats

The provision for providing reservation for the Scheduled Castes, the Scheduled Tribes and women in me total number of sects for the members and the offices of chairperson of the Panchayats at all levels was mandatory and, therefore, all the States have made the necessary provisions for the same in their relevant Acts. However, the matter of reservation for The Backward Classes was open and it was left to the State Legislatures to decide. In Article 243 D (6) of the Constitutional Amendment it was mentioned that "Nothing in this part shall prevent the

Legislate of a State from making any provision for reservation of seats in any Panchayat or offices of chairpersons in the Panchayats at any level in favour of Backward Class of Citizens'. It was really a difficult task for the States to take a decision in the matter and, therefore, there is no uriformity in the provisions made by various States in this regard.

The States of Assam, Kerala, Orissa, Tamil Nadu and West Bengal have not accepted the idea of reservation for backward classes in the Panchayats. In Punjab only one seat of member and that too only in such Panchayats where the population of backward classes is over 20 per cent in the Panchayat area shall be reserved for the backward class of citizens and in case of chairperson there shall be no reservation at all for such classes. More or less the same position exists in Haryana. In Gujarat only one-tenth of the total seats in the Panchayats at various levels shall be reserved for socially and educationally backward classes and there shall be no reservation for the backward class of citizens as such. In Madhya Pradesh 25 per cent of the seats shall be reserved in such Panchayats only where the reservation for the Scheduled Castes and the Scheduled Tribes is 50 per cent or less.

In Madhya Pradesh there is also a provision that if the chairperson does not belong to the Scheduled Castes, the Scheduled Tribes or the OBCs, the Deputy Chairperson shall be elected from amongst the members belonging to such classes or tribes. In case of Maharashtra, 27 per cent of the total seats shall be reserved for the Backward Classes and in Andhra Pradesh and Karnataka about one-third of the total seats shall be reserved for such classes. In Bihar, Himachal Pradesh, Rajasthan and Uttar Pradesh the reservation shall be according to their proportion of the population in the concerned Panchayat area. However, in case of Uttar Pradesh such reservation shall not exceed 27 per cent of the total seats.

(viii) No-Confidence Motion Against the Chairperson

Almost in all the States there is a provision to remove the Chairperson at all levels through a no-confidence motion to be passed by the elected members. There is, however, some variation from State to State as regards the procedure and the requisite number of elected members required to pass such a resolution. It could be seen from the Annexure that in case of Haryana the chairperson can be removed only if the motion is carried out by at feast 2/3rd members of the Gram Sabha in a special meeting where at least half of the members should be present and a notice for such a motion will be accepted only if it has been signed by at least 2/3rd of the members of the Village Panchayat. In Haryana and Punjab also the chairperson can be removed by the members of the Gram Sabha only. In Madhya Pradesh the chairperson can be removed only if the no-confidence motion is camed by at least 3/4th of the elected members. On the other hand in Himachal Pradesh the chairperson can be removed by a no-confidence motion carried by a simple majority of the elected members.

However, in other States the Chairperson can be removed through a no-confidence motion carried by at least 2/3rd of the elected members of the Panchayat. In case of Tamil Nadu the Inspector on his own or at the request of 2/3rd of the total members of the village Panchayat shall call a meeting of the village Panchayat for the purpose and the inspector can remove the chairperson in view of the opinion of the members.

(ix) Composition of the Panchayat at the Intermediate Level

The Legislature of a State was also free to provide for the representation of the Village Panchayats in the Panchayat at the Intermediate level. Similarly the Legislature was to decide whether to provide or not for the representation of the members of the House of People and the members of the Legislative Assembly of the State concerned representing constituencies which comprise wholly or partly the Panchayat area and the States were also free to take a similar decision regarding the representation of the members of the Council of States and the members of the Legislative Council of the State who are registered, as voters in the concerned Panchayat area.

Regarding the representation of the chairpersons of the village Panchayats in the Panchayat at the intermediate level, there is a great variation. In Gujarat, Madhya Pradesh and Maharashtra there is no representation of the chairpersons of the village Panchayats in the Panchayat at the intermediate level. In case of Karnataka, Himachal Pradesh and Rajasthan, one-fifth of the chairpersons of the village Panchayats shall be represented in the Panchayat at the Intermediate level by relation for one year in case of Tamil Nadu and Haryana chairpersons of the Village Panchayat equal to one-fifth of the total elected members of the Panchayat at the intermediate level shall be elected by rotation to be represented in the Panchayat at the intermediate level. Punjab has also adopted more or less the same pattern. However, in case of rest of the States all the chairpersons of the Village Panchayats shall be represented in the Panchayat at the intermediate level.

The State-wise position of the composition of the Panchayats at the intermediate level.

A. Representation of the Chairpersons of the Village Level Panchayat

I. State where all the chairpersons of the village level Panchayats shall have representation:

1. Andhra Pradesh, 2. Assam, 3. Bihar. 4. Kerala, 5. Orissa, 6. Uttar Pradesh, 7. West Bengal.

II. States where only one-fifth of the chairpersons of the village level Panchayat shall have representation on rotation basis for one year:

1. Himachal Pradesh, 2. Karnataka, 3. Rajasthan.

III. States which have adopted a different pattern:

1. Punjab (Sarpanches and elected members in the ratio of 40: 60)

2. Tamil Nadu (1 /5th of the elected members).

3. Haryana (equal to 1/5th of the total seats in the Panchayat at the Intermediate level)

IV. States where the chairpersons shall have no representation:

1. Gujarat, 2. Madhya Pradesh, 3. Maharashtra.

B. Representation of MPs, MLAs and MLCs

(i). States where MPs, MLAs and MLCs (where Legislative Council exists) have representation:

1. Andhra Pradesh, 2. Assam, 3. Bihar, 4. Haryana, 5. Himachal Pradesh, 6. Karnataka, 7. Tamil Nadu, 8. Uttar Pradesh, 9. Uttarakhand (10) West Bengal.

(ii). States where only MLAs and MLCs have representation:

1. Kerala, 2. Gujarat, 3. Madhya Pradesh, 4. Orissa, 5. Punjab, 6. Rajasthan.

C. Norms for Electing Members Directly on Constituency basis

(i) One member for every 15 thousand population—Punjab.

(ii). One member for every 10 thousand population—Karnataka.

(iii). One member for every 5 thousand population—

1. Bihar, 2. Madhya Pradesh, 3. Tamil Nadu.

(iv). One member for every 4 thousand population—Haryana.

(v). One member for every 3 thousand population—Himachal Pradesh.

(vi). One member for every 2 thousand population—Uttar Pradesh.

(vii). Number of members fixed:

1. Assam (one member from each Gram Panchayat).
2. Gujarat (15 members upto one lakh population and two members for every additional 25 thousand population).
3. Kerala (number between 8 and 15).
4. Maharashtra (one member from each electotal college).
5. Orissa (one member from each Grama).
6. West Bengal (number not exceeding three from each Grama),

(viii). No norms defined under the Act—1. Andhra Pradesh, 2. Rajasthan.

Surprisingly, there is no uniformity in case of

representation of the MPs, MLAs and MLCs in the Panchayats at the Intermediate level. In Kerala, Gujarat, Madhya Pradesh, Orissa, Rajasthan and Punjab there is no-representation for MPs at the intermediate level. However, rest of the States have provided representation for them. There is also no uniformity regarding the status of such members. In Rajasthan the MLAs and the chairpersons of the Village Panchayats have the status of permanent invitees and they do not have a right to vote in the meeting of the Panchayats. In Andhra Pradesh also the chairpersons of the village level Panchayats shall have the status of permanent invitees. There is also no uniformity regarding the number of members to be elected directly in the Panchayat at the Intermediate level.

There shall be one member for every 15 thousand population in Punjab, 10 thousand population in Karnataka five thousand population in Bihar, Madhya Pradesh and Tamil Nadu, four thousand in Haryana, three thousand in Himachal Pradesh and two thousand in Uttar Pradesh. Some of the States have fixed the minimum and maximum number of members to be elected directly for the Panchayat at the Intermediate level. In Punjab the number shall vary between 6 and 10, in Madhya Pradesh between 10 and 30. In Orissa and Assam there shall be one member from each Gram Panchayat and in West Bengal there shall be members not exceeding three from each village.

(x) Composition of the Panchayat at the District Level

The norms in terms of population for deciding the number of members to be elected directly for the Panchayat at the district level vary from State to State. However, the actual position at a glance is as follows.

A. States where chairpersons of the Intermediate Level Panchayats shall have no or partial representation in the District Level Panchayat:

1. Gujarat, 2. Madhya Pradesh, 3. Tamil Nadu (Chairman of the Panchayat Union Council equal to 1/5th of the elected members of the District Panchayat to be elected).

B. State having no representation of the Members of Parliament—Gujarat.

C. Norms for electing members directly on constituency basis:

(i) One member for every 50 thousand population: 1. Bihar, 2. Madhya Pradesh, 3. Punjab, 4. Uttar Pradesh.

(ii) One member for every 40 thousand population:

1. Assam, 2. Haryana, 3. Karnataka, 4. Orissa.

(iii) One member for every 20 thousand population: Himachal Pradesh.

(iv) Number prescribed: 1. Andhra Pradesh (one member from each Mandal Parishad).

2. West Bengal (not exceeding three members from each block).

3. Gujarat (17 members upto a population of 4 lakhs and two members for every additional one lakh population).

4. Kerala (number between 10 and 20).

5. Maharashtra (number between 40 and 60).

(v) No norms defined under the Act—1. Rajasthan, 2. Tamil Nadu.

Remarkably, in Bihar, Madhya Pradesh, Punjab and

Uttar Pradesh there shall be one member for every 50 thousand population. Similarly in Haryana, Karnataka, Assam and Orissa there shall be one member for every 40 thousand population. In Andhra Pradesh one member and in West Bengal upto three members from each Panchayat at the intermediate level shall be elected directly for the District Level Panchayat. In Gujarat there shall be 17 members upto a population of four lakhs and two members for every additional one lakh population. In Maharashtra the number of directly elected members shall vary between 40 and 60 and in case of Kerala it shall vary between 10 and 20.

Regarding the representation of the chairpersons of the Panchayats at the intermediate level in the District Level Panchayat except for the States of Gujarat and Madhya Pradesh all States have provided for their representation. However, in case of Andhra Pradesh and Rajasthan they shell be treated as permanent invitees only.

In case of Tamil Nadu only such number of chairpersons of the Intermediate level Panchayat which shall be equal to one-fifth of the elected members shall be elected to represent the Panchayats of the intermediate level in the District Level Panchayat. As regards the representation of the MPs except for Gujarat all States have provided for the same. In Gujarat only the MLAs shall be represented and that too they shall have the status of permanent invitees only having no voting rights at all.

Committee System

Remarkably, one of the important aspects of Panchayati Raj Institutions is the structure of committees through which the PRIs perform most of their functions. The Committee system is not altogether new in Indian rural local bodies, it existed from the time when the Panchayati Raj structure was established in the country. The Panchayati Raj bodies at various levels have to discharge a wide range of functions as the general body in most cases is too large a body to meet regularly and to deal with the matters assigned to them effectively. Hence, the need for committee system. The Constitutional Amendment is, however, silent on the subject, yet every State has provided for the standing or functional committees.

(a) Village Panchayat Level Committees

The number of committees, their composition, structure, scope and functions vary from State to State. As regards the number of committees, it varies from two to five. Orissa has provided for as many as five committees followed by Uttar Pradesh which has provided for four committees. Many of the States have provided for three committees, the States of Assam, Bihar. Haryana, Himachal Pradesh, Karnataka and Punjab come under this category. Gujarat and Kerala have provided for three committees each.

In Andhra Pradesh in addition to a committee known as Beneficiary Committee, the Gram Sabha may constitute functional committees for agriculture, public health, sanitation and communication. The States of Madhya Pradesh and Maharashtra have left the matter to the Village Panchayats to constitute standing committees according to their requirements and the Panchayati Raj Acts of Tamil Nadu Rajasthan, and West Bengal are silent on the subject. As regards the number of membership of the Standing Committees in different States it varies from two to six. In almost all cases the members of the Committees are to be elected by the elected members of the Panchayat and in most cases the Chairperson or the Deputy Chairperson of the Village Panchayat shall perform the duties of the chairman of the Standing committees.

The major functions of the committees can be categorised broadly into two heads—(a) Production and sectoral development programmes like agriculture, animal husbandry, rural industries, education, health, public works, poverty alleviation programmes etc.; and (b) Programmes concerning the welfare of the weaker sections including protecting them from social injustice and exploitation.

(b) Committees at the Intermediate Level

Notably, barring for Andhra Pradesh and Maharashtra all the States have provided for standing committees at the intermediate level. In Andhra Pradesh a Mandal Panchayat may, and if so required by the Government shall, join with other local authority in constituting a Joint committee for any joint purpose. The Maharashtra Act is silent on the subject. The number of committees varies from State to State ranging between 2 and 7. West Bengal having as many as seven committees tops the list. Madhya Pradesh, Orissa and Rajasthan having five committees each come next. Uttar Pradesh and Tamil Nadu have four Committees each followed by the States of Assam, Bihar, Haryana, Himachal Pradesh, Karnataka and Punjab having three committees each. Gujarat and Kerala have provided for two Committees each only. The number of members to be included in these committees varies from 3 to 9 and all the members have to be elected by the elected members of the concerned Panchayat. For example the Administrative Committee in Tamil Nadu shall have only three members against seven to nine members in each of the seven committees constituted in West Bengal.

However, in most of States the number of membership

varies from five to six. In most cases the Chairperson or the Deputy Chairperson of the concerned Panchayat shall act as ex-officio chairman of these committees. However, in case of West Bengal, Gujarat and Madhya Pradesh most of the committees shall elect their own chairman.

(c) Committees at the District Level

Again, except for Haryana every State has mentioned in their respective Acts the names of the committees to be constituted at the district level. In Haryana the matter has been left to the Zilla Parishad to constitute such committees as it may deem necessary. As regards the number of committees it varies from State to State. West Bengal has provided for as many as eight committees against only four in Assam. Andhra Pradesh, Gujarat and Maharashtra have provided for seven committees each; Uttar Pradesh six and Kerala, Rajasthan, Tamil Nadu, Punjab, Madhya Pradesh, Karnataka and Bihar five committees each. As regards the number of members it ranges from 5 to 17. However, most of the States have five member committees. In Assam, Bihar, Himachal Pradesh, Karnataka, Madhya Pradesh, Punjab, Rajasthan and Tamil Nadu each committee shall have members not exceeding five.

On the other hand in Maharashtra the Standing Committee shall have 16-17 members and the rest of the committees also shall have 8 to 10 members each. Similarly in Uttar Pradesh Karya Samiti shall have 10 to 13 members and rest of the committees shall have 6 to 9 members each. In many states most of the committees are headed by the chairperson of the District Panchayat. In West Bengal except for one committee the rest of the committees shall elect their own chairman.

In most cases the Chief Executive Officer of the District Panchayat shall be the ex-officio Secretary of the Standing Committees. As regards the term and conditions of membership there is no uniformity. For example in Bihar and Maharashtra no member shall serve on more than one committee, in Punjab, Karnataka, Tamil Nadu and Assam two committees and in Himachal Pradesh three committees.

Power and Functions

Basically, the status of any institution or organisation is determined by its powers and functions. Under the Indian Constitution local government has not been recognised as a distinct layer of authority like Union and State Governments. According to the division of powers and functions under the Constitution, local government fails within the legislative list of the State Governments. Accordingly, the range of functions to be discharged by local bodies is entirely at the discretion of the State Governments.

Prior to the Seventy-Third Constitution Amendment Act, 1992 the powers and functions assigned to the Panchayati Raj bodies in different States were largely based on the broad recommendations of the Balwantrai Mehta Committee. The Committee emphasised that the functions of the Panchayati Raj bodies should include all areas concerning social and economic development of the area in a general sense. In particular, the Panchayati Raj Institutions should be entrusted such functions like public health, clean water, lighting, cleansing, local roads and amenities.

To these the development programmes should be added like agriculture, animal husbandry, fisheries, social forestry, rural industries, family planning, education, social education, welfare programmes, irrigation channels, rural electrification and so on. Regarding the allocation of functions between different tiers, the Mehta Team had favoured a strong Panchayat Samiti (the Panchayat at the intermediate level) and a non-executive coordinating Zilla Parishad at the district level.

The Team suggested that all the functions concerning a village within the jurisdiction of a Village Panchayat area should be the responsibility of the Village Panchayat except for the functions involving common interests of mete than one Village Panchayat. The functions where more than one Village Panchayats are involved should be discharged by the Panchayat Samiti. Similarly, such functions of the Panchayat Samiti as may involve more than one Panchayat Samitis should be the responsibility of the Zilla Parishad. In spite of Balwantrai Mehta Committee's preference for the Panchayat Samiti to play a vital role, in the total scheme of Panchayati Raj System, this approach was not viewed with favour by all States and many of the States favoured a strong Zilla Parishad. In the third meeting of the Central Council of Local Self-Government, the Local Government Ministers of West Bengal and Uttar Pradesh, showed definite bias towards the Zilla Parishad. Similarly Naik Committee in Maharashtra and Mysore Resources and Economy Committee observed that the District Level was not sufficiently emphasised in the scheme of Mehta Report.

It was felt that the District Development Council should be made a prime democratic local body with not only control and supervision over the Intermediate and Village level Panchayats, but with wide functions and powers to take up and execute all development works and plan schemes upto the District level. Rajasthan had adopted the pattern of a strong Panchayat Samiti model.

But after an experience of the working of the system for some years the State had a rethinking on the subject and had appointed a Study Team to look into the matter. The Study Team did not favour a Strong Panchayat Samiti model and recommended that a significant change is necessary in the functions and powers of the Zilla Parishad in order to activise and vitatise them. The Ashok Mehta Committee also examined the subject in greater detail and felt that decentralisation should be genuine and adequate; it should be regarded as a functional necessity, and not as an act of political charity. The Committee recommended that the developmental functions relating to a district, that are now being discharged by the State should be decentralised to the Zilla Parishad level. Such would be in agriculture and allied sectors, marketing, health, education, communication, rural industries, welfare of backward classes, family welfare and the like. According to the Committee, certain exceptions such as research in agriculture, college and University education, medium irrigation projects involving complications or items covering a larger area than one district, pilot projects etc., will naturally have to be with the State Government. The Committee furtner emphasised that when a function is assigned to the Panchayati Raj bodies, it should also be understood that the Panchayats should have the corresponding money components also with them for discharging such functions efficiently and effectively.

The Committee added that such of the regulatory functions, which are very closely allied with developmental work may also be assigned to the respective tiers of Panchayati Raj Institutions as part of the work programme specifically entrusted to them. The Workshops of District Magistrates/Collectors on Responsive Administration recommended that the Constitutional provision dealing with Panchayati Raj Institutions should also delineate the subjects that are to be dealt with at the district level. It would be preferable to have a clear cut lists spelling out the subjects with the State Government and those that are to be handled at the district level.

The Workshops felt that the subjects like agriculture, animal husbandry, fisheries, cooperation, minor irrigation, social welfare, hearth and family welfare, primary education, drinking water in rural areas, rural development, adult education, relief works during natural calamities, social forestry, rural roads, rural electrification and non-conventional sources of energy should be handled by the Panchayati Raj Institutions. The Workshops emphasised that the functions and activities stemming from each of these subjects should be further spelt out with reference to the level and the agency which would deal with a given functional activity. A perusal of the pre-Seventy-Third Constitution Amendment position of Panchayati Raj Acts of different States shows that the functions entrusted to Village Panchayats in most States included provisions and maintenance of civic services, pubic hygiene, maintenance of public works, primary education, agricultural production, rural industries, primary heath care, women and child welfare etc.

The functions of the intermediate level Panchayats were very limited including various local schemes entrusted to them and some works taken up from their own resources, The District Panchayats were generally advisory and funds distributing bodies. except in a few States where fairly substantial funds were placed at their disposal for taking up district level schemes. A number of studies have, however, pointed out that the Panchayati Raj Institutions have generally shown more interest in agency functions than their statutory functions.

Some studies have also emphasised that the Panchayati Raj Institutions have great potential and can very well shoulder the responsibility of planning and implementing development projects relating to economic development and social justice. Under the Seventy-Third Constitution Amendment it has been left to the States to endow the Panchayats with such powers and authority as may be necessary to enable them to function as institutions of self-government. However, the Amendment casts a duty upon the States that the devolution of powers and responsibilities to Panchayats may contain provisions in respect to:

(a) the preparation of plans for economic development and social justice,

(b) the implementation of schemes for economic development and social justice as may be entrusted to them including those in relation to the matters listed in the Eleventh Schedule.

In fact, the Eleventh Schedule of the Constitution 29 subjects have been listed and the State Legislatures were required to decide the specific nature and type of activities and schemes to be carried out by different tiers of the Panchayats. It is obvious that while assigning these functions to different tiers of Panchayats, the cardinal principle for distribution of powers and functions at each level of Panchayats must be that what could be done at the lower level should be assigned to that level alone and not to the higher level.

Further it would not be enough to merely list out the subjects, there must be clear delegation of powers to each level of Panchayats for discharging their functions effeciently and effectively.

Remarkably, study of the Panchayati Raj Acts of different States which have been enacted after the Seventy-Third Constitution Amendment Act, 1992 reveals that there is no uniformity in assigning the functions to different levels of Panchayats. There are three types of models which emerges in this regard.

1. States which have drawn the list of functions and activities for different levels of Panchayats in a routine manner on the lines of the subjects listed in the Eleventh Schedule. In such States, in addition to the functions included in the Eleventh Schedule, some general functions like preparation of annual plans, consolidation of the plans prepared by the lower level of Panchayats, preparation of annual budget, providing relief in natural calamities, organising voluntary labour, promotion of unity and harmony in the society, maintenance of essential statistics, removal of encroachment on roads etc., have also been added to the list. The States of Assam, Bihar, Haryana, Karnataka, Punjab, Rajasthan and Uttar Pradesh fall under this category. In these States no priority of functions has been identified and the Panchayats have to perform all functions according to the availability of funds.
2. States where functions have been categorised under two heads: (a) Obligatory or mandatory functions; and (b) Discretionary functions. In the category of

obligatory functions more essential activities have been included and in this case it shall be the duty of the Panchayat concerned to carry out such functions. In the second category of functions such activities have been included which a Panchayat may perform subject to the availability of funds. Such States are Orissa, Kerala, Gujarat, Tamil Nadu and West Bengal.

3. States which have drawn their own list, of course, keeping in view the subjects listed in the Eleventh Schedule. Such States are Andhra Pradesh, Himachal Pradesh, Maharashtra and Madhya Pradesh.

Notably, some of the experts are of the opinion that mere listing of functions in the Act will not serve the purpose. A detailed exercise would be necessary for identification of schemes to be carried out by the Panchayats at various levels under each sector as they are reflected in the budget document. For identification of the schemes each concerned department at the State level will have to follow the cardinal principle that a scheme which can be easily handled by a Panchayat of the lower level should only be entrusted at that level alone and not to the higher level body. Similarly a fresh thinking has to be made as to which of such schemes that at present are under the State sector can be transferred to the Panchayat sector. It would be worthwhile to constitute expert groups for the purpose in each State and the matter should not be left to the department concerned alone. The representatives of the department concerned and Panchayati Raj Institutions and experts should be included in the Group.

Financial Resources

Under the Constitution of India, unlike Union and

State Governments, the local government do not have any independent powers of taxation. The local Government institutions derive their powers of taxation and raising their resources from the State Legislature. The fiscal status of the States has to a large extent determined the fiscal status of the local bodies. It is felt that the States themselves have very limited resources at their disposal, in fact while making division of resources between the Union and States, the States have had the initial disadvantage of losing some of the lucrative tax heads. The ones which were entrusted to the States are not elastic or buoyant. Their power of independent borrowing also is severely circumscribed..

Hence the States have become increasingly dependent on the Centre for resources. States which look to the Centre for their resources can neither ensure fiscal independence of the local bodies nor transfer adequate resources to enable them to perform the functions deploying on them. It is argued that the weak foundations on which Local Government finances were built, one could say that the grassroots of democracy in India have always been undernourished. In view of the concentration of resources in the Centre, the scarcity of finances is felt at the State and more autcely at the level of local bodies. The State Governments which are already short of funds can not provide the local bodies with adequate resources required for discharging their responsibilities.

No doubt, in the past, in almost all the States, the Panchayati. Raj bodies were empowered to levy certain taxes, impose fees on selected activities and raise their own resources. But if is strongly felt that they have, by and large, failed to make full use of their powers of taxation etc. Various studies have shown that even the States of

Maharashtra. Gujarat, Andhra Pradesh and West Bengal, which are considered relatively better in this regard, have not been able to levy taxes or fees on more than two or three items which included profession tax, special tax on tands and buildings and fax on public entertainments.

On the whole, the overall financial position of the Panchayati Raj bodies in most of the States remained unsatisfactory. The Ashok Mehta Committee observed that the Gram Panchayats in different States, except for Kerala, are usually without resources adequate to function as per the expectations of the people.

The data compiled by the Committee show that the average annual income of Gram Panchayats differs from State to State and Kerala has the highest average income of a lakh of rupees per Panchayat. The average income per Gram Panchayats in Maharashtra, Gujarat, Andhra Pradesh, Tamil Nadu and Assam ranges between 9 and 13 thousand rupees and in Rajasthan. Karnataka, Orissa and Himachal Pradesh it ranges between rupees 4 and 6 thousand. It is shocking that in U.P. the average annual income per Gram Panchayat was less than one thousand rupees. In terms of per capita basis, the annual income of all Panchayats from all sources works out to 61 paise per capita in Uttar Pradesh against Rs. 8. 41 in Maharashtra, Rs. 7. 11 in Gujarat, Rs. 5. 61 in Kerala, Rs. 4. 56 in Andhra Pradesh and Rs. 3. 78 in Tamil Nadu. The Committee observed that generally the present Panchayats are not viable. The size of the Panchayats should permit the effective discharge of the functions decentralised by Government; it should present a viability criterion which will include harnessing of the several economic flows that are becoming patent, and also facilitate the satisfaction of the welfare requirements. According to the Committee, the concept of constituting Panchayat for each village is against the criterion of viability. The position of financial resources of the Panchayat Samitis is more or less the same in all the States, except in the case of Maharashtra where these bodies do not have a corporate status and thus no funds of their own. In case of Maharashtra the funds with the Samitis are generally grants from Zilla Parishad while in other States the funds are basically the finances provided to the block for Commmunity Development programmes and other activities.

According to the Committee, the Zilla Parishads rarely raised their own resources and depended mainly on grant from the Government. In Maharashtra the Zilla Parishad have substantial powers of taxation, but few districts have utilised these powers. Against this a major portion of receipts of Zilla Parishads in U.P. is from taxes and revenue receipts. The Committee felt that in spite of all the exhortation on the need to raise their own resources by way of taxation, there is a general reluctance on the part of Panchayati ' Raj institutions to impose taxes.

This reluctance is visible not only in the case of Village Panchayats, which are in face-to-face contact, with the people but also in case of Zilla Parishads even in such States as Maharashtra where they are performing a variety of developmental functions and need additional resources.

The Committee thus felt that the need for some taxes being made binding upon the Panchayati Raj Institutions is self evident. Some scholars have suggested that the Gram Panchayats may altogether be relieved of the power of taxation and that they should exclusively depend upon the grants from the higher level institutions.

The argument behind this logic is that the Gram

Panchayat is too small an institution to maintain an elaborate administrative arrangements to assess and efficiently collect the taxes. On the other hand, several scholars do not agree to this line of approach and emphasise that in case the Gram Panchayats are divested of powers of taxation and are made to survive on the external support, it will lose the shadow of power that it should enjoy.

The Balwantrai Mehta Committee had contemplated that almost the entire development work of rural areas will be the charge of the Panchayat Samiti (the Panchayat at the middle level) and recommended that the following sources of income should be assigned to them:

(a) A statutorily prescribed percentage of land revenue, the land revenue assigned to the Panchayat Samitis and the Village Panchayats should not be less than 40 per cent of the total land revenue of the State.

(b) Such cess on land revenue, water rate for certain minor irrigation works etc., as is leviable under the various Acts.

(c) Tax on profession, trades, callings and employment should be levied by the Panchayat Samitis and not by Village Panchayats.

(d) Surcharge on duty on the transfer of immovable property.

(e) Rents and profits accruing from properties like ferries, fisheries etc.

(f) The net proceeds of tolls and leases on roads and bridges etc.

(g) Pilgrim tax.

(h) 'Tax on entertainments including amusements,

(i) Proceeds from periodical fairs and markets, bazaars, hats and mandies.

(j) Primary education cess,

(k) A share of motor vehicle tax.

(l) Voluntary public contributions,

(m) Grants made by Government.

The Committee felt that in case of some of the above taxes, it will be necessary to prescribe a compulsory minimum rate. According to the Committee, the Village Panchayats will have the following as their main resources:

(a) Tax on daily, bi-weekly or weekly markets, bazaars, hats etc., whether located on private land or otherwise.

(b) Property or House Tax.

(c) Tax encarriages, carts, bicycles, rickshaws, boats, and pack animals.

(d) Octroi or terminal tax.

(e) Conservancy tax.

(f) Water rate.

(g) Lighting rate,

(h) Income from cattle ponds,

(i) Fees to be charged for registration of animals sold within the local area for the use of sarais, slaughter houses etc.

(j) Grants from Panchayat Samitis.

The Committee was of the opinion that in case of Village panchayats also it will be necessary to prescribe a compulsory minimum rate in respect of some of the above taxes.

Under the Seventy-Third Constitutional Amendment the State Governments are required to make suitable provisions with regard to financial viability of Panchayati Raj bodies. While doing so the State Government ought to give due consideration to the fact that the association of Panchayati Raj Institutions in development process can not be meaningful unless there are sufficient funds with them for management of local affairs. The State legislature is supposed to devolve responsibilities, powers and authority to the PRIs both to enable them to function as institution of self-government and also to prepare and implement plans and schemes of economic development and social justice.

The State legislature is obliged to transfer to the PRIs necessary finances and/or financial powers. The financial resources contemplated for the PRIs at various levels are to be as laid down in Article 243 H of the Constitution. According to this Article, the legislature of a State may, by law:

(a) authorise a Panchayat to levy, collect and appropriate such taxes, duties, tolls and fees in accordance with such procedure and subject to such limits;

(b) assign to a Panchayat such taxes, duties, tolls and fees levied and collected by the State Government for such purposes and subject to such conditions and limits;

(c) provide for making such grants-in-aid to the Panchayats from the Consolidated Fund of the State; and

(d) provide for constitution of such Funds for crediting all moneys received respectively by or on behalf of the Panchayats and also for the withdrawal of such moneys there from, as may be specified in the law.

Obvionsly, under the Constitution the PRIs do not have any independent financial powers and it is the State legislature which has a final say in the matter. It is the State legislature which may authorise a Panchayat to levy, collect and appropriate any tax, duties, tolls and fees. Even the procedures and limits of the taxes, duties, tolls and fees placed at the disposal of the PRls have to be prescribed by the State legislature.

In case of assigning to a Panchayat such taxes, duties, tolls and fees which are levied and collected by the State Government, the State legislature may also decide the conditions and limits and same is the case with regard to providing grants-in-aid to the Panchayats from the Consolidated Fund of the State.

The basic question that arises in regard to financial devolution relates to the conditions the State legislature may impose on PRls even in matters where PRls are authorised under the Acts, to levy, collect end appropriate taxes etc. Does it not go against the principle of autonomy of the self-government? Ideally speaking, the PRIs should have independent powers to raise resources of their own.

However, in this case also there is a danger that the PRls may not mobilise the resources for the simple reason of earning unpopularity. It would thus be better if some taxes etc. are made obligatory which the PRIs have to levy and collect. In this connection some safeguards in the form of incentives and disincentives may also be prescribed. In the past also some States had sought to encourage Gram Panchayats to increase their tax yield. Gujarat had a Gram Encouragement Fund in each district out of which grants were to be paid to Panchayats raising tax rates or levying new taxes. Gram Panchayats in Tamil Nadu received from the State Government a grant equal to actual house tax collected.

In many other States also cash prizes were given for outstanding performance in tax collection or resource mobilisation. A State-wise list of the taxes, fees, duties and other sources of income placed at the disposal of Panchayati Raj bodies as compiled from the Acts of different States. While preparing the list of the most common sources of income which are generally available to the Panchayats almost in all the States have not been included in the above list. Some of such sources are shares of taxes and other revenues as determined by the State Finance Commission, contribution and grants made by Government or higher level Panchayats or other local authorities, loans and borrowings by the State Government or the Central Government or other financial institutions, donations, sales proceeds, gifts and contributions, penalties, income from endowments, rent or profit from property, fees for use or occupation of buildings etc.

Formation of State Finance Commission

Remarkably, the Seventy-Third Constitution Amendment the functional decentralisation has been made through the Eleventh Schedule under which a broad list of functions has been provided which the Panchayati Raj Institutions are expected to perform but the matter of financial devolution has been left to the State Legislatures. However, according to the Constitutional Amendment every State has to constitute a Finance Commission which shall review the financial position of the Panchayats and make recommendations to augment their resources. Under Article 243 H of the Constitution it has been provided that the Governor of a State shall, as soon as may be within one year from the commencement of the Constitution (Seventy-

Third Amendment) Act, 1992 and there after at the expiration of every fifth year, constitute a Finance Commission to review the financial position of the Panchayats and to make recommendations to the Governor as to:

(a) the principles which should govern:

(i) the distribution between the State and the Panchayats of the net proceeds of the taxes, duties, tolls and fees leviable by the State, which may be divided between them under this part and the allocation between the Panchayats at all levels of their respective shares of such proceeds;

(ii) the determination of the taxes, duties, toils and fees which may be assigned to, or appropriated by the Panchayats; and

(iii) the Grants-in-aids to the Panchayats from the Consolidated Fund of the State;

(b) the measures needed to improve the financial position of the Panchayats;

(c) any other matter referred to the Finance Commission by the Governor in the interest of sound finance of the Panchayats.

The Governor shall cause every recommendation made by the Commission together with an explanatory memorandum as to the action taken thereon to be laid before the legislature of the State. Through Constitution (Seventy-Third Amendment) Act, 1992 a sub-clause (b) has also been inserted in Article 280 of the Constitution. According to this sub-clause, the Central Finance Commission, in addition to other recommendations, shall make recommendations to the President as to the measures needed to augment the Consolidated Fund of State to supplement the resources of the Panchayats in the State on the basis of the recommendations made by the Finance Commission of the State. The legislature of the State may, by law, provided for the composition of the State Finance Commission and the qualifications which shall be requisite for appointment as members thereof and the manner in which they shall be selected. In compliance of the Constitutional Amendment all the States have constituted Finance Commissions.

It would appear from the Annexure that in case of Madhya Pradesh, Maharashtra and Punjab no details regarding the composition and qualification, for members have been provided in their Acts. In each State the Commission shall be headed by a Chairman and shall consist 3 to 5 members including chairman except for Haryana where a provision of one or more members has been made. It is notable that large States like Uttar Pradesh and Bihar have smaller Finance Commissions consisting only 3 members each.

As regards the qualifications prescribed for the appointment of the Chairman of the Commission the States of Assam, Bihar Haryana, Karnataka, Tamil Nadu and U.P. have not provided any detail in their respective Acts. In case of Andhra Pradesh, Gujarat and Rajasthan the qualification laid down for the Chairman include a persons having experience in public affairs. In case of Orissa it has been pointed out that if it is impracticable to appoint a person having experience in public affairs as chairmen a member of Council of Minister of State shall be appointed as Chairmen.

Remarkably, task of the State Finance Commissions is to make sure that adequate finances are made available to the Panchayati Raj Institutions so that they can discharge their duties and perform their functions properly. However, there is a great fear in the minds of many that in view of the scarce resources of the States it may not be possible for the State Finance Commissions to allocate sufficient funds as would be required by the Panchayati Raj bodies for discharging their responsibilities properly.

The State Finance Commission would make recommendations for the devolution of finances and/or financial powers to the Panchayati Raj Institutions and if is on the basis of the recommendations of the Commissions that not only will the State Governments make financial allocations to the Panchayati Raj Bodies but also the Central Finance Commission will consider measures to supplement the finances of the State Governments. It is understood that the Tenth Finance Commission has taken a note of this and some funds have been earmarked for the purpose as required under Article 230 (3) (bb) of the Constitution. In the context of the role of the Finance Commissions, I.S. Gulati in his article on the subject has brought out many valid points. He has rightly pointed out that when a State Finance Commission deliberates the question of providing Panchayati Raj Bodies at various levels with adequate funds, the matter of adequacy cannot be determined without considering the functions and responsibilities of the Panchayati Raj Institutions and it would be the State legislature, and not the State Finance Commission, which has to decide as to what specific functions and responsibilities it is willing to transfer to the Panchayati Raj Bodies.

The State Finance Commission has then to decide and recommend such devolution of funds and/or financial powers to enable the Panchayati Raj bodies to discharge those functions and responsibilities satisfactorily. However, the broad guidelines in the form of the Eleventh Schedule have already been laid down through the Constitutional Amendment and the State legislature has to identify the specific schemes and activities to be carried out by the Panchayati Raj Bodies at various level keeping in view the overall frame work of the Eleventh Schedule. As regards the specific terms of reference of the State. Finance Commissions, each State has to decide in its own way under the overall frame-work of the general guidelines laid down by the Constitutional Amendment in this connection Unlike the Constitutional provisions regarding the Central Finance Commission the terms of reference of the State Finance Commissions would be more comprehensive as it will not restrict tax sharing to any specified tax or duty levied at the State level. In other words the State Finance Commissions will not be obliged to confine its recommendations on revenue sharing only to certain specified taxes or duties. Gulati has cautioned that keeping in view the challenging task of the State Finance Commission, the State legislature need to be more careful in making appointments to the Commission of persons whose competence.

Integrity and objectivities are fully established and known in the State. It would, no doubt, greatly enhance the credibility and acceptability of the Commission if persons of eminence in the field are appointed as chairmen and members of the Commission. It would also be better if a senior serving officer having experience of finance and local bodies may be appointed as the wholetime Secretary of the Commission as is the practice at the national level. As regards the scope of the State Finance Commission in the matter of plan and non-plan funds, the Constitutional Amendment do not draw any distinction between the plan and non-plan financial requirements of the Panchayati Raj Bodies. There is no reason, therefore, why the State Finance Commission should feel bound to confine themselves to the assessment of non-plan expenditure of local bodies for recommending the devolution of funds and financial powers to the Panchayati Raj Bodies at various levels. What a State Finance Commission has to ensure is that the Panchayati Raj bodies are given access to funds which enable them to perform satisfactorily the functions, developmental or non-developmental they are assigned.

District Planning Committee

The subject of economic and social planning, being a matter of common interest to the Union and the States, has been appropriately placed in the Concurrent List of the Constitution of the country. Under the Directive Principles of the State Policy it has been laid down that the State to promote the welfare of the people by securing protecting, as effectively as it may, a social order in which justice, social, economic and political, shall inform all the institutions of the national life. The State shall in particular, strive to minimise the inequalities in income, and endeavour to eliminate inequalities in status, facilities and opportunities, not only amongst individuals but also amongst groups of people residing in different areas or engaged in different vocations.

The achievement of this objective calls for planned development of the country. Till recently the formulation of plans in its real sense was limited to the Union and State levels and the concept of decentralised planning is of a recent origin. The Sarkaria Commission has rightly pointed out that the *raison detre* of decentralised planning is the better perception of the needs and resources of local areas, facilitating more informed decisions to be taken.

It gives local people a greater say in decision making about their own development and welfare, resulting in better coordination and integration of various programmes at the local level. It also leads to greater mobilisation of resources of the community and at the same time inculcates the spirit of self-reliance in the local people, 'involvement of the local people results into fuller exploitation of the growth potential of the area, improved productivity and increased production. With the participation of the local people the assets created are also maintained more efficiently. The Hanumantha Rao Working Group on District Plan has pointed out that the District Plans so far have been conceived as rural plans only. According to the Group, with the introduction of the IRDP and the new orientation in planning there is a need to integrate the rural activities with the plans of the urban areas, particularly with the of the small and medium towns.

The small and towns have to function as focal points for agricultural activities and for the provision of higher order services and amenities such as marketing facilities, banking services, housing, repair workshops, recreation and the like. The working Group, therefore, recommended that towns with a population of less than 10,000 should be treated as an integral part of the District Plan for purposes of overall planning and implementation of development programmes in the district.

With such integration, it is also necessary to ensure that the funds provided at the State level for urban development sector are duly disaggregated on a proportional basis for such towns for meeting the cost of urban services into the rural framework of the District Plan. According to Article 243 ZD of the Constitution, there shall be constituted in every State at the district level a District Planning

Committee to consolidate the plans prepared by the Panchayats and the Municipalities in the District and to prepare d draft development plan for the district as a whole.

The legislature of a State may, by law, make provision with respect to:

(a) the composition of the District Planning Committee;

(b) the manner in which the seats in such committees shall be filled. Provided that not less than four-fifths of the total number of members of such committee shall be elected by and from amongst, the elected members, of the Panchayats at the district level and of the Municipalities in the district in proportion to the ratio between the population of rural areas and of the urban areas in the district;

(c) the functions relating to district planning which may be assigned to such committees;

(d) the manner in which the chairpersons of such committees shall be chosen.

Every District Planning Committee shall, in preparing the draft development plan:

(a) have regard to—

   (i) matters of common interest between the Panchayats and the Municipalities including spatial planning, sharing of water and other physical and natural resources, the integrated development of infrastructure and environmental conservation;

   (ii) the extent and type resources whether otherwise;

(b) consult such institutions and organisations as the Governor may, by order, specify.

The chairperson of every District Planning Committee shall forward the development plan, as recommended by such Committee, to the Government.

Though the provision of the District Planning Committee has not been made in the Seventy-Third Constitution Amendment, the new Panchayati Raj Acts were expected to provide for the details in respect of the constitution of the District Planning Committee so that the provisions of the Seventy-Fourth Constitution Amendment may be met.

Out of the 16 States under study only 6 States (Assam, Bihar, Himachal Pradesh, Karnataka, Rajasthan and Tamil Nadu) have provided some information in their Acts. No State has mentioned the manner in which the elected members shall be chosen. Similarly no State has provided the list of specific functions which the District Planning Committee shall perform.

As regards the composition of the District Planning Committee all the 6 states which have provided the details have opted for more or less the same pattern. In addition to the directly elected members, MPs, MLAs, MLCs, Chairperson of the Zilla Parishad, Mayor or Chairman of the Municipal Corporation/Municipal Board having jurisdiction over the Head Quarter of the district have been included in the District Planning Committee.

In Bihar and Assam the chairperson of the District Panchayat shall be the ex-officio chairman of the District Planning Committee and in case of Himachal Pradesh, Karnataka, Rajasthan and Tamil Nadu the State Government have yet to take a decision in the matter.

State Control

The PRI in India have never been recognised as the third-tier of the Government, it was neither the intention of the Constitution of the country. Being a subject matter under the State List, the Legislature of the State has exclusive power to make laws with respect to the constitution and powers of the local bodies. Under the circumstances the local bodies will always be subordinate to the State Government and shall be accountable to the legislature of the State. Thus there is a full justification for exercising necessary State control over the working of the local bodies. The State Governments have the power to frame laws and rules for the smooth functioning of the local bodies.

The State Governments also have the powers of suspension and dissolution of the local bodies under certain conditions and for a fixed period. However, within the given frame work the State Governments are expected to allow the local bodies to function as the effective units of self-government. The intention of the Constitution of the country is also that the State Governments should provide full autonomy to the local bodies to work within the general framework of the Acts passed by the State Legislature in this regard. The various studies have however, shown that in the past, unfortunately, this has never happened and in most of the States the Government kept the local bodies, particularly the rural local bodies under suspension or dissolution for decades.

No norms were followed in this regard and in most cases such actions of the State Governments were mostly arbitrary and politically motivated. Most of committees and working groups which have examined the subject in depth have suggested that some safeguards should be provided against the misuse of the power of the State

Government to suspend or dissolve the Panchayati Raj Bodies and for this purpose some objective norms should be prescribed under the Acts for taking this extreme step of suspension or dissolution. Each case of suspension or dissolution should be discussed at proper forums.

In case it becomes necessary to suspend or dissolve a Gram Panchayat, the matter should be examined thoroughly by the Zilla Parishad and the Government should take this extreme step only when such a resolution is passed by not less than 2/3rd members of the concerned Zilla parishad. Similarly in case of suspension or dissolution of a Panchayat at the intermediate or the district level the resolution of suspension or dissolution should be passed by a majority of members of the Legislative Assembly of the State. Further, in case of suspension or dissolution of a Gram Panchayat the concerned District Magistrate should conduct the enquiry and the report of the District Magistrate should be submitted to the Zilla Parishad.

Similarly in case of suspension or dissolution of the Panchayat at the intermediate or the district level the Commissioner of the division should conduct the enquiry and submit his report to the Government. Under the Constitution (Forty-Third) Amendment Bill, 1977, the power of suspension or dissolution of a Panchayat was proposed to be vested with the Governor. To be more specific, under the Bill it was proposed that if at any time the Governor of a State is satisfied that any Panchayat in that State is not functioning in accordance with law or is grossly abusing its powers or is functioning in a manner which is detrimental to public interests, he may suspend or dissolve the Panchayat and appoint an Administrator to exercise the powers vested in the Panchayat.

Every order of suspension or dissolution together with resolutions therefore shall be laid before the legislature of the State and shell cease to operate at the expiration of six weeks from the reassembly of the Legislative Assembly of the State, unless before the expiration of that period, it has been approved by a resolution of the State Legislative Assembly. An order made under this clause may be withdrawn at any time by the Governor. An order so approved by the legislature shall unless revoked, cease to operate at the expiration of six months from the date of passing the resolution approving the order and an election to constitute the Panchayat shall be completed before expiration of the said period. With the Seventy-Third Amendment the problem of keeping a Panchayat in the stage of suspension or dissolution for a long period has been solved as now it is obligatory for the State Government to have elections conducted within six months of the dissolution of a Panchayat.

Inspection

In all the States the Government have, by and large, got the powers of inspection, supervision and control of Panchayats. In most cases, an officer of the State Government duly authorised by it in this behalf may inspect all books and proceedings and records and he is also authorised to enter on and inspect any work in progress of a Panchayat.

In all the Acts it has been clearly mentioned that the office bearers, the officers and servants of the Panchayat shall be bound to afford access to all such information and records as may be demanded by the inspecting authority. In Gujarat the office bearers of the higher level Panchayats are also authorised to make inspection of the Panchayats at the Village level. In Maharashtra and Karnataka the

Chief Executive of the Zilla Parishad, in West Bengal Inspector, in Haryana Director/CEO, in Kerala Commissioner, in Tamil Nadu Inspector/Collector/ Government and in rest of the States the Government or any person or officer authorised by the Government have got the powers of inspection of the affairs of the village Panchayats. Similarly in case of the Panchayat at the intermediate level, in Haryana Director/CEO, in Karnataka CEO, in Kerala and Maharashtra Commissioner, in West Bengal Inspector, in Tamil Nadu Inspector/Collector/ Government, in Orissa and Uttar Pradesh the D. M. / Prescribed Authority and in rest of the states the Government or any person or officer empowered or authorised by the State Government have got the power of inspection of the activities of the Panchayats at the intermediate level.

Power of Dissolution

Almost in all the States the Government have got the powers of dissolution of Panchayats. If at any time it appears to the State Government or the prescribed authority that a Panchayat is persistently making default in the performance of the duties imposed on it by or under the Act or under any other law for the time being in force, or exceeds or abuses its powers or fails to carryout any orders of the State Government or the prescribed authority, the Government or the prescribed authority may, after such enquiry as it may deem fit, dissolve such Panchayat and may order a fresh constitution thereof.

However, no such order shall be passed unless reasonable opportunity has been provided to the concerned Panchayat for furnishing its explanation. The position regarding the power of dissolution of the Panchayats also varies from State to State. As regards the Village

Panchayats, in Bihar the Zilla Parishad or the Government, in Karnataka and Maharashtra the Commissioner, in Himachal Pradesh and Madhya Pradesh the Prescribed Authority or the Government and in rest of the States the Government have got the powers of dissolution of the Village Panchayats. In case of the Panchayats at the intermediate and district levels, in Himachal Pradesh and Madhya Pradesh the Prescribed Authority or the Government and in rest of the States the Government or any person or officer authorised or empowered by the Government have got the powers of dissolution of the Panchayats at the intermediate and district levels. In case of dissolution of a Panchayat, in all the States the Government have got the power to make ad hoc administrative arrangements to conduct the affairs of the concerned Panchayat and its committees, in Bihar the zilla Parishad and in Karnataka the Zilla Parishad or the Government may appoint any person/persons/committee to perform the functions of the Panchayats. In Tamil Nadu the Government may empower the Panchayat Union Council to look after the functions of the Village Panchayat and in Kerala an Administrative Committee or a Special Officer and in Rajasthan an Administrator may be appointed for the purpose.

On dissolution of Panchayat under this clause the following consequences shall follow:

(a) all the office-bearers end members of the Panchayat shall vacate their offices;

(b) all powers and duties of the Panchayat snail, untill the Panchayat is reconstituted be exercised and performed by the Government or such person or persons or committee of persons as the State Government or the prescribed authority may appoint in this behalf.

A Panchayat so dissolved shall be reconstituted within six months of its dissolution and such reconstituted Panchayat shall function for the remaining term of the Panchayat for which the dissolved Panchayat would have continued had it not been so dissolved. However, if the unexpired period is less than six months the reconstitution of Panchayat would not be necessary for this period.

The State Government may, from time to time, cause an inquiry to be made by any of its officers in regard to any Panchayat on matters conerning it or on any matter with respect to which the sanction, approval, consent or order of the State Government is required under the Act. every member, office bearer, officer or servant of Panchayat shall be personally liable for loss, waste or misapplication of any money or other property of the Panchayat to which he was a party or which has been caused by him by misconduct or gross neglect of his duties.

Suspension of the Execution of Resolution/Works

The State Government or the prescribed authority may suspend the execution of any resolution passed, order issued license or permission granted or prohibited by a Panchayat, if in its opinion—

(a) such resolution, order, licence, permission or act has not been legally passed. Issued, granted or authorised;

(b) such resolution, order, licence, permission or act is in excess of the powers conferred by the relevant Act or is contrary to any law; or

(c) me execution of such resolution or order, or the continuance in force of such licence or permission or the doing of such act is likely—

(i) to cause loss, waste or misapplication of any money or damage to any property vested in me Panchayat;

(ii) to be prejudicial to the public health, safety or convenience;

(iii) to cause injury or annoyance to the public or any class or body of persons; or

(iv) to lead to a breach of peace.

As regards the authority as to who can suspend the execution of resolution passed by a Panchayat or the works to be carried or undertaken by a Panchayat the position. It would appear from that in case of a Village Panchayats in Gujarat the Taluka Development Officer or the DDO, in Man/one the DOO or Panchayat Officer or SDO (civil), in Rajasthan and Karnataka the CEO (subject to confirmation from Government), in Tamil Nadu the Inspector, in Punjab the Director, in Assam and Bihar the Zilla Parishad (subject to confirmation from Government), in Maharashtra the Standing Committee of the Zilla Parishad and in rest of the States the Government or the Prescribed Authority have got the power of suspension of execution of any resolution/work of the Village Panchayat.

In case of the Panchayat at the intermediate level in Gujarat the DDO or the Collector, in Karnataka the Commissioner, in Maharashtra the D.M. or the Commissioner, in Rajasthan the CEO, in Tamil Nadu the inspector and in the rest of the States the Government or the Prescribed Authority have the power of suspension of execution of resolution/work of the Panchayat.

Regarding the District Panchayats, in Gujarat the Collector or the officer authorised by Government, in

Maharashtra the D.M. or the Commissioner, in Punjab the Director, in Rajasthan the CEO, in Tamil Nadu the Inspector and in rest of the States the Government or the Prescribed Authority have got the power of suspension of resolution/ work of the District Panchayat. In almost all the States there is a provision that if in the coinion of the Executive Officer of a Panchayat any procasal or resolution of the Panchayat is violative of, or .inconsistent with the provisions of the Act or any other law, it shall be his duty to bring the same to the notice of the concerned Panchayat for its reconsideration and he shall not implement such order or resolution.

Suspension and Removal of the Chairperson

In almost all the States the Government or the prescribed authority may suspend from office any office bearer of a Panchayat against whom charges have been framed in any criminal proceedings and who has been served with a notice along with a charge sheet to show cause for his removal from office. When any inspection or any audit discloses the misappropriation, misutilisation or embazzlement of Panchayat funds by an office earer of a Panchayat and when the prescribed authority is satisfied that continuance in office of such a person will prejudice the enquiry and apprehends tampering with record and witnesses, the Government may suspend such a person from office. The State Government or the prescribed authority may also after such enquiry as it may deem fit to make at any time, remove an office bearer:

(a) if he has been guilty of misconduct in the discharge of his duties or abuses his power; or

(b) if he refuses to act or becomes incapable of acting or is adjudged an insolvent; or

(c) if his continuance in office is undesirable in public interest.

Provided that no person shall be removed unless he has been given an opportunity to show cause as to why he should not be removed from his office. However, as regards to the authority as to who can suspend or remove a chairperson differs from State to State.

In case of the power of removal of the chairperson of the Village Panchayats, in Bihar, Gujarat, Himachal Pradesh, Madhya Pradesh, Rajasthan, Kerala, Uttar Pradesh and West Bengal the Government or any person or officer empowered or authorised by the Government or the prescribed authority or the competent authority have got this power. In Punjab the Director, Panchayats and in Haryana the Director or the Deputy Commissioner have got this power. In Andhra Pradesh this power has been given to the District Collector, whereas in Karnataka the Commissioner and in Tamil Nadu the Inspector have got this power.

The cases of Assam and Maharashtra are of a different type. In Maharashtra the Standing Committee of the Zilla Parishad have got the power of removal of the Chairperson of the Village Panchayat. In respect of the Chairperson of the Panchayat at the intermediate level in the States of Andhra Pradesh, Gujarat, Haryana, Himachal Pradesh, Madhya Pradesh, Punjab and Rajasthan the Government or any person or officer empowered or authorised by the Government or the competent authority or the prescribed authority have got the power of his suspension and in the Acts of rest of the States there is no mention in this regard. As regards the power of removal of the chairperson at this level, except for Assam, the Government or the person or officer empowered by it or the Competent authority or the Prescribed Authority have got his power. However, in Assam the Zilla Parishad with the approval of the Government can remove the chairperson of the Panchayat at the intermediate level.

Regarding the suspension of the chairperson of the District Panchayat, the Government or the person or officer empowered by the Government or the competent authority or the Prescribed Authority have got this power in almost all the States. However, in the Acts of Assam, Bihar, Karnataka, Kerala, Maharashtra, Tamil Nadu, Uttar Pradesh and West Bengal there is no mention in this connection.

As now (April 2010), we are at the threshold of passing the Womens Reservation Bill of earning their quota in the Parliament and state legislatures, let us hope for a dawn of new era.

7

Womenpower and Rural Development

"The wheel that squeaks the loudest
Is the one that gets grease."

—John Billings

We all know that most of the population lives in village in India and agriculture is the main stay of live. A major portion of our womenpower is engaged in agriculture and allied activities. Rural woman are the most deprived community of our society. As such if we are really serious to enhance the status of women, we have to make concerted efforts at rural development in integrated manner.

Here in the present chapter we will make an attempt to address the pertinent issues of womenpower in the context of agriculture and rural development.

It is pertinent to note that current situation in developing countries in agriculture, food production and rural development derives from a historical pattern of development in which investment has been skewed in favour of industrialisation and urban areas with the result that in the majority of countries rural areas have lagged behind in their development.

In Africa, Latin America, the Middle East and certain

parts of Asia the development paradigms pursued so far have created food shortages and a structural cleavage in rural society. The resultant rural transformation has led to a cleavage between commercial or large-scale agriculture, which has been rapidly modernised through application of scientific and technological innovations, higher capital investment with higher returns, and small scale subsistence agriculture with little or no capital investment and a low level of technology, requiring high labour inputs with low and even declining returns. Such developments in agriculture have sometimes been due to the need to earn foreign currency.

Furthermore, this cleavage has taken the form of a gender differentiation in which men predominate in the decision making and management of commercial or large-scale agriculture, while women continue to predominate in the food and subsistence sector in which they expend large amounts of labour—as evidenced by the long hours of work with low levels of technology and low returns. Moreover, within commercial agriculture the gender division is also reflected by the high demand for female labour in those cycle of production requiring hoe and hand methods (e.g., weeding or paddy transplanting) with low remuneration. This cleavage has meant that many developing countries have not been able to attain the goal self-reliance in the areas of food, agriculture and rural development.

A substantial number of countries continue to experience a severe decline in food production, leading to food shortages and even outright hunger and famine. Moreover, even in countries which have been able to expand their food sectors, the system of distribution is inadequate and poverty, hunger and malnutrition still afflict large masses of the people.

According to the FAO, malnutrition and hunger increased by 15 per cent during the seventies, affecting 450 million people in Asia, Africa and Latin America. In developing market economies as a whole, daily per capita calorie consumption has remained at 2 per cent below the minimum requirement.

The gap is largest in Africa, followed by South and South-East Asia. In Sub-Saharan Africa, the growth rate of agricultural production fell to 1.3 per cent annum while population growth remained at 27 per cent over the second development decade. (Acharya, 1984, pp. 1-2). South and South-East Asia have witnessed a rise in the cost of food production, falling rural employment and landlessness, the latter being particularly marked among rural women. Structural changes in many Latin American countries have led to unemployment and lack of entitlement to food among large sections of the population, including the most vulnerable section, namely those involved in subsistence agriculture. Women in developing countries are a major resource in agriculture, food production and rural development, as evidenced by their numerical proportions, their share of labour in agriculture and food production and the division of labour by sex in this sector. Their share of labour is particularly significant in view of the fact that in many cases they perform their agricultural work in addition to long and arduous work in child-care household maintenance, cooking and fuel wood collection, as well as food preparation and processing.

Despite women's crucial role in agriculture and food production their potential for accelerating rural development has not often been well understood or appreciated. Inherited biases in the agrarian development approaches have led to an inadequate perception of women's economic role, undercounting or devaluation of their work and thus to a perpetuation of the dependency of developing countries on external factors of production. Since agricultural productivity in the developing countries for many years to come must depend on the quality of human labour, it is imperative to recognise that the farm that insufficient attention has been devoted to the improvement of the productivity of labour is a major constraint to agricultural development. In practice, women have not benefitted from adequate policy support.

First of all the accumulated evidence suggests that agrarian and land tenure policies have restricted women's access to land and other factors of agricultural production, such as technology, credit subsidy and inputs (e.g. fertilisers and seeds). Secondly, women have not had equal access to support services and incentive system for expanding agriculture, food production and rural development, for instance, extension and training services and information. Thirdly, lack of an integrated approach to development at the national level has consistently perpetuated a fragmentary approach to women's position in the society and their role in development, thereby perpetuating the promotion of women's programmes through social welfare, humanitarian and demographic approaches only, without provisions for long term integration. In traditional societies women's role in agriculture and food production was recognised by customary rights of access to land, forests, and to support from family labour.

Structural changes under colonialism and in the post-colonial phases have eroded many of these rights, but the responsibility of feeding the family still rests primarily with the women in many rural communities of Africa and in the economically least affluent sections of many Asian and Latin American societies. The privatisation of land and the introduction of cash crops for domestic and foreign markets, the need to feed expanding populations, and the depletion of forest resources for industrial and communications growth, which were initiated during colonialism and continued after independence, have steadly reduced women's access to basic resources.

The withdrawal of male labour—for deployment in mining, roads and railway building, plantation of export crops and new industries—which was initiated by colonial regimes also increased women's burdens. Despite international recognition of rural women's right to own land (World Conference on Agarían Reform and Rural Development-Rome, 1979), attempts to incorporate this principle in land tenure and land development policies have been marginal.

Forest policy, including policies for reforestation has yet to recognise the role of women in forest development, even though in some areas women have initiated major protest movement against deforestation which have negatively affected their ability to feed their families and livestock. Case studies from Asia and Africa indicate that rural women are very dynamic and innovative in these fields when they are give the opportunity to participate collectively in such developmental activities.

They also indicate a process of increasing self- confidence among women and an enhancement of their status within their families and the community. However, extension of such experiments to other areas will require uncorporation of women as a target group in policies and structures for agarian reform, and development of forests, agriculture, animal husbandry, silk production, fish culture, land development (including waste lands) etc.

Unless the structural constraints and the existing 'invisibility' of women in rural development policies and agrarian reform are removed, it is difficult to envisages an equitable growth and expansion of agriculture, food and forest production. It is important to take specific short-run measures to make them sensitive to women's potentials and the promotion of research and communication programmes for rural women in these areas.

However the solution to the problem lies in the establishment of long-term strategies and measures to implement them as a matter of national priority in the context of solutions to, for example chromic food problems deforestation and ecological imbalances, unemployment and poverty, and to enhance the process of corrective and individual self-reliance.

Apparently, new initiatives are needed to reorient agricultural policies at the national level which would give priority to a balanced approach to agricultural communities and food production.

Within this policy restructuring process, a number of specific issues arise. These include:

(1) creating a balance between export production for foreign exchange purposes and food production in such a way that women can directly benefit from their labour in food and commercial agriculture;

(2) achieving better treatment for materials exported to the world market and better marketing opportunities for them;

(3) changes in commodity pricing accompanied by subsidy arrangements to compensate farmers for crop failure and market fluctuations;

(4) creation of opportunities for equitable access to land for women;

(5) increasing investment in research on food crops, especially drought resistant cereals (in particular sorghum and millet) and legumes. Experiments in these areas should enlarge the knowledge base already amassed by food farmers and agricultural societies. In this way, research can permote and benefit from endorgenous bases of knowledge in food farming which in many cases has had the advantage of long and well-tested results.

A food strategy might be designed to support rural development and agrarian reforms and other relevant measures for strengthening and food sector recommended, for example, by the World Conference on Agrarian Reform and Rural Development or the Lagos Plan of Action for African Development. Since food strategies are relatively new initiatives, whose policy guidelines are still being drawn up, they could provide an important policy intervention to strengthen women's role in food production.

Here it is pertinent to note that in view of the role of women in farming and the inadequacy of access to services for expanding production the following measures could be fruitful:

1. savings and investment programmes should aim at providing credit, finance and subsidies for women through various channels:
   (a) regular agricultural financing institutions and credit programmes could include the elaboration of specific mechanisms for assisting farm women; and
   (b) revolving funds and credit subsidies extended to women through their associations net-works, and local level groups, as well as government offices at the local level, in conjunction with

information campaigns to encourage women to use these services.

(2) current farmer training programmes, including the ECBC TCDC programmes, could be reviewed and modified to cater for women farmers. An important elements of adjustment here would be to provide agricultural training programmes which would increase women's technical knowledge and allow them to combine mothering and training opportunities;

(3) new organisational schemes, especially those at the community level should be extended through women's groups and associations:

(4) increasing women's competence to participate in rural institutions, decision making and designs for agricultural and food programmes.

The persistence of the subordinate position of women in society, as illustrated by the experience in the agriculture and food sector, is a negation of the goals of development, which affects ill members of society equally, regardless of sex or creed. Conversely, the elimination of sex-based inequality could constitute a legitimate basis for innovating approaches to the implementation of the objective of self-reliance and provide an opportunity to test integrative development in practice.

Application of Technology

From the point of view of the importance of industrialisation, the pattern of industrialisation adopted in developing countries is most relevant. Differences in the socio-economic environment of individual developing countries resulted in various industrialisation strategies. However, regardless of the different industrialisation policies and practices of the individual developing countries, they have a common desire to generate national product, promote employment and secure the most dynamic possible modernisation, so as to secure a greater degree of technological and financial independence from the developed countries.

The level and the features of the industrialisation of developing countries are usually determined by the individual country's resources, both material and human, and by its past experience of development. The great dependence of the industrialisation processes in developing countries or developed countries, on technology transfer, capital investment, export markets, etc., has resulted in a high degree of exploitation and in unbalanced industrial structures which are highly sensitive to international economic fluctuations.

Thus, the introduction of new industries and changes. In the industrial structure of a developing country may profoundly and rapidly influence the overall economic structure. Such influences may bring about unexpected or unplanned changes unplanned and social life. Developing countries often find it difficult to fully control the structural changes in their industries and thus avoid industrial instability and exploitation of the workforce. This may to some extent be possible for those countries which have large internal markets, strong public sectors, or were able to control investments in industrial development through generation of sufficient internal funds.

The industrialisation processes in developing countries have also been affected by transnational corporation from the developed countries, which often see industrial development in developing countries as a means of transferring obsolete and unclean technologies, or as a means of increasing profits through redeployment of labour-intensive industries. This has particularly affected the position of women, since their employment in the industrial sector has greatly increased, without, however, securing legally recognised working conditions protection, remuneration, etc.

About two thirds of the net increase in the female industrial workforce (the number of women employed in industry in the world increased by 104 per cent in the last two decades) took place in developing countries mainly in Asia. In contrast to Africa and Latin America, Asia has a higher share of the female than of the male world industrial labour force (UNIDO, pp. 3-4). However, for an appropriate assessment of the improvements in the field as analysts of the qualitative aspects of such employment is needed.

Generally, women are engaged in labour-intensive industries with low productivity (e.g. processing industries—textile, food, leather, etc.). Their wages are influenced by their poor bargining position, and they have no influence at all on working conditions. Thus, for instance, although the working hours in manufacturing have generally tended to decline, in some developing countries working hours have tended to rise. The treatment of the female labour force is to a large extent a reflection of women's low status on the labour market (reserve labour army), lack of proper education and training low or non-existent organisation, the lack of or non-implementation of protective legislation (particularly in export-oriented industries) and their generally unfavourable social position.

The recent upward trend in women's employment in developing countries is not very significant in relation to the absolute size of the female population or workforce in these countries. Moreover, although this increase is in some of the most modern industries in the world, it does not appear to have made a substantial difference to women status, since it has done little to break the isolation and discrimination of women in the industrial workforce. The extension of the practice of subcontracting of home workers for certain stages of industrial production processes may have considerable counter-productive consequences, for women's formal employment.

Such organisational changes may sometimes lead to a circumvention of legal protective measures for labour, a deterioration of working conditions, lower wages within and outside industry, greater exploitation of women's and children's labour, diminishing union activity and, in the long run, also to increased formal unemployment of both men and women. While the short-term positive effects of income generation cannot be discounted, the negative effects of channeling or restricting women's employment to the informal sector make it considerably more difficult and could lead to a higher degree of isolation, exploitation and inequality of women, by excluding them from the mainstream of socioeconomic activity. It is unlikely that the position of women in the industries of developing countries can be changed without changes in the models of industrial development and organisation of industrial production. Therefore, formulation and implementation of national industrialisation policies based on the needs and interests of all strata of the population, as well as on an evaluation of domestic potentials continue to be priority tasks confronting developing countries. The existing potentials of developing countries are certainly conducive to positive changes.

Balanced development planning and policies which

aim at maximum utilisation of national resources and at an expansion of domestic demand are also the proper framework for the advancement of the role of women in this sector of the economic and for promotion within overall development.

To improve women's position in industry, a number of measures would have to be incorporated in the industrial policies of developing countries:

(1) legal arrangements covering all aspects of industrialisation, from investment codes to regulations, which would provide for better general treatment of labour in industry. In this connection, there should be regulatory measures in free exporting zones to ensure that social costs are also covered. However, it must be recognised that collective action by the developing countries is needed for the successful legislation and implementation of such measures;

(2) changes in education, which would enable women to improve their position in industrial employment, and to acquire transferable skills through various forms of vocational and informal training;

(3) extention of employment opportunities in accordance with human resources development policies;

(4) strengthening of self-reliance in industrial policy through industrial cooperation among developing countries, exchange of information and experience through ECDC/ TCDC programmes and projects.

(5) adoption of technologies which ensure stability of employment and professional progress to women workers;

(6) establishment of overall social control and of schemes for genuine workers' participation in management and decision making;

(7) elaboration of criteria for determining the size of enterprises in various industrial branches and the ways of organising them; promotion of small and medium-size enterprises in developing countries; establishment of industrial cooperatives;

(8) selection, development and transfer of technology and know-how as well as training of personnel;

Certainly, this would improve the bargaining position of developing countries *vis-a-vis* developed ones, particularly in case of transfer of technology or foreign investment, in enforcement of national legal mechanisms for the protection of the industrial labour force, including women workers. All this calls for urgent action among developing countries in the field of industrialisation.

BASICALLY, developing countries have, relatively poor scientific and technological capacities at their disposal. The promotion of science and technology in these countries thus requires strong international communications and a pooling of the existing scientific knowledge and technological potential, in line with the developmental needs of developing countries. The main issue connected with the utilisation of science and technology as a pool to speed up the development of the developing countries is, therefore, the transfer of technology and, in this respect, the choice of technology. Technology being a system consisting of hardware, software and orgware, the transfer of technology must be viewed as a complex process, involving a range of economic, financial, legal and sociological factors. In this connection, local inputs—primarily knowledge and information on technologies, trained cadres, legal and other regulations, etc.—are needed.

The process of selection of technologies calls for an analysis and assessment not only of the economic impact, but also of the social impact. It must be kept in mind that while technology itself is natural, the application of technology can have considerable social effects, since, through technology, a system of domination and exploitation, as well as a set of social norms and ethics may be transferred. A social impact analysis should be a constituent part of any transfer of technology arrangement.

This analysis should specifically consider the impact of technology on women family and community life and other social and cultural values of the new environment to which the technology will be transferred. Women are involved in science and technology through the structural transformations that occur with the transfer of technology and scientific and technological development, and as participants in research and technological activities; and experiencing the impact of the technologies on their everyday lives. In all cases, their involvement should be much stronger than it is at present. It is also very important that women understand scientific and technological innovations, because this enables them to influence the general social attitudes towards technological change through the existing non-formal education.

The radical changes in the organisational pattern and activities of the society, associated with rapid scientific and technological change in the overall organisation, which are presently being experienced in the developed countries, may also dramatically affect all developing countries, and lead to either a more dynamic and humane development or to an ever higher degree of dependency and exploitation. The problem of the marginal position of some members of society, and of women specifically, cannot be solved unless the elements of these new technologies can be built into development strategies in accordance with the concept of integral development.

Furthermore, the latest so-called frontier and transdisciplinary technologies can be used in different ways and at different levels. Their use can serve to accontuate the productive role of women, because such technologies are applicable to a number of areas which are of relevance to the betters quality of life and to the integration of women in development, i.e. food production, clean water supply, improved housing conditions, use of alternative energy sources, in the services education etc.

Such technologies also stimulate the growth of employment, as they offer a variety of employment combinations. However, it should be kept in mind that it is economic and political considerations, rather than social and cultural ones, which determine the availability and terms and conditions for the access of developing countries to new technologies and which are important for national development. Women's access to technological development thus also depends on the global relations between the technology owners and users and those who try to secure access to new technology and to processes of industrialisation. This implies that major efforts should be made to maximise the utilisation of the existing knowledge in developing countries and to lessen the technological dependence on developed countries.

Women have traditionally gained knowledge and experience (e.g., in agricultural production, energy utilisation, running the household, manufacturing objects for everyday use, home medicine etc.,) which have not been, exploited from the developmental point of view. The application of new scientific and technological devices and knowledge may lighten household drudgery in urban and rural areas, providing better water, energy and other community facilities.

This would release energies which women might be encouraged to direct forwards active and useful participation in other economic and social areas, and in the overall technological transformation of the society.

Remarkably, greater involvement of women in scientific and technological development would therefore require:

(1) an increase of the level of scientific and technological self reliance by developing national scientific and technological potentials, maximisation of the possibilities for technical proporation among developing countries and the introduction of selective transfer of technology systems.

(2) popularisation of scientific and technological knowledge and skills in order to enable their further development, by mass media, through changes in school programmes, and through all participatory and community development activities.

(3) changes in the traditional attitudes towards women by enabling them to fully participate in scientific and technological development by stimulating their involvement in various forms of education and training.

(4) establishment and strengthening of cooperation among developing countries in the areas of information on scientific and technological knowledge and devices transfer of technology and exchange of experience on application of science and technology in development, joint research, etc.

(5) establishment of linkages between the existing traditional technologies and know-how and the new technologies. The involvement of women in the strengthening of these links could provide a firm basis for self-reliance and ensure a certain continuity in the development of authentic and original approaches, thus avoiding imitative modernisation, and developing participatory research as well as relating scientific and technological development to the specific needs of the country.

Skills and Services

In fact, the analysis of the role of women in the services sector covers the generally complex problem of services classification and data, the identification of the manpower problem in general, and women's hidden economic role in particular, and the relationship between the services sector and the overall economy of the country. Over the last decades this sector's contribution to GDP increased substantially, not only in developed market economies but also in developing countries, where this upward trend was evident even in the least developed countries.

By 2000, the services sector accounted for the largest share of GDP in both developed market economies as well as in developing countries. However, the expansion of the services sector in developing countries, particularly in least developed countries, is probably due to quite different economic causes and could the attributed to the marginalisation of the labour force in agriculture and industry. The development of services is partly due to major changes in agriculture and industry, and partly to their heterogenous production and consumption characteristics.

The role of women in the tertiary sector is very difficult

to determine. However, the distribution of the female labour force may serve as an indicator. In 1980, 66.3 per cent of the total female labour force in developing countries was employed in agriculture, 16.3 per cent in industry and 17.4 per cent in services. This is very different from the situation in developed countries, where the shares are 13.7 per cent for agriculture, 29.0 per cent for industry and 57.3 per cent for services.

In developing countries the share of females in the total labour force, by economic sectors, was highest in agriculture (36.4 per cent, even with universed figures) and much lower in the services sector (26.9 per cent) and industry (26.5 per cent). There are considerable disparities between developing countries in the different regions—disparities between Latin America on the one hand and Asia and Africa on the other. In Asia the main feature is the relatively high share of women in the total labour force in industry (28.8 per cent) and the lower share in services (23.2 per cent). In Latin America the low share of women in the total agricultural labour force (9.3 per cent) is in sharp contrast to the situation in the other two regions. In this region female employment in the services sector is as high as 38.3 per cent. In Africa women account for 31.6 per cent of labour in services, while their share in industry is only 19.7 per cent. (UNIDO, 1984).

In relation to the integration of women in development some partial issues arising in the service sector have been studied. These include trade (women being active internal trade, mostly in the petty trade of the informal sector); transport (links between rural and urban areas, developed and underdeveloped regions, formal and informal sectors); banking (mainly in connection with the problems of access to credit); tourism (increased opportunities for productive employment, provision of lodging, catering, etc., could discourage some negative forms of tourism).

Many of the service activities in which women are employed do not require formal technical qualifications. Other activities such as health (especially nursing) and education (especially teaching) do require professional qualifications, but these are in many cases considered an extension of the essentially female role which has its origin in the household—the mother care offered to the family.

Thus women's contribution in this sector has not really been adequately recognised. No doubt much of the productive activity of women in the services sector remains invisible because of its mainly traditional and informal nature in developing countries. Some thought should be devoted to the services which this sector could provide to meet the needs of households in this countries, that is, what the services sector should produce for the household and its members.

From the point of view of the importance of the role of women in this sector and of the significance of the services sector for the improvement of the status of women in developing countries, it is suggested that:

(1) services classification and data collection should be made more transparent and accessible;

(2) attention be paid to the analysis of the functioning, growth and development of the services sector (both public and private) in all developing countries, especially as regards the interlinkages among this and all other sectors;

(3) the position of women in this sector should be viewed as developmental and integrative of other activities,

which means that the new developmental trends observed in this sector must be closely linked to overall development and the advancement of women;

(4) could be pursued with a view to the development of self-reliant schemes. Cooperation among developing countries in this sector could contribute to exchange of experiences, to development of self-reliant schemes and linkages between micro and macro levels of implementation. This may be an avenue for the promotion of new approaches to the development of the services sector.

(5) cooperation among developing countries in this sector, which is scattered over different areas and usually invisible being traditional and informal;

(6) women's hidden economic role in the services should be further studied and analysed.

Admittedly, Education is a double-edged instrument: it can contribute to and be an ally of structural changes in society by training people in required skills—old, newly emerging and anticipated. It is also a value-generating process—influencing the behaviour, norms and cultural attitudes of people, particularly younger ones. From the beginning of the movement for the equality of women in recent history, great emphasis was placed on education as the major instrument for the elimination of gender inequality. Developing countries have viewed education as an instrument to stimulate development in all fields, and to reduce their dependence on external advisers.

The basic problems were to promote a rapid expansion of development and cultural structures to meet the manpower requirements of development and cultural progress in general. Scarcity of resources and the shifting priorities of development have constrained the balanced pursuit of these aims. One of the objectives which had a low priority in the allocation of efforts and resources was the elimination of gender inequality. Illiteracy still remains a major problem in most developing countries and women constitute a large proportion of the illiterates.

About 60 per cent of the approximately .800 million adult illiterates in developing countries today are women. Although the proportion of illiterates in the total adult population has decreased, the results are still unsatisfactory. The absolute number of illiterates in these countries is still increasing. Gender differences persist among illiterates, especially because the lower enrolment ratios for girls at the elementary level increase the number of illiterate women. Trends in the process of equalising the access of men and women to different levels of the educational system, as measured through enrolment ratios, show some interesting results. Over two decades (1960-80) the gender gap in enrolment ratios for the age groups 6—11 and 12— 17 has remained virtually constant in developing countries, although there is overall improvement in entrolment for both sexes. At the higher level of education, the gap is much narrower, in contrast to developed countries, where the gender gap exists mainly at the higher level.

At this level the gender gap has shrunk in the developed countries during the last decade, and it has slightly widened in the group of developing countries. (Sicherl, 1984). The persistence of these gaps prevents the equalisation of educational opportunities with consequent effects on employment, skill acquisition and participatory opportunities in all fields. The widening of the gap in higher education is a matter of serious concern, because this sector is the training ground for entry into many areas important development, *e.g.*, science and technology, communication industries utilising high level technology, professions such as law, medicine, etc. It is also the training ground for most managerial and decision-making occupations.

The participation of women in decision-making positions, which is already limited, could shrink still further if this gap were to expand. In addition to resource constraints, educational progress in developing countries has been impeded by many other problems. Lack of harmony with productive and other developmental activities, which is often a consequence of borrowed models of educational systems, imposed the need to reform and adapt educational systems and institutions, to turn increasingly to the informal aspects of education (vocational training, on the job-training, etc.), and to introduce mass media and other modern devices as useful means of spreading educational programmes and contents in an effort to reach as many social groups as possible.

Developing countries have been experiencing great problems in education, reflected in poor material basis and functional difficulties, in sometimes alarming drop-out levels (especially in Sub-Saharan Africa and South Asia), in the fact that a substantial proportion of children are unable to read and write even after going to primary school for four or five years, etc. Women are still mostly employed in traditional and informal sectors where there has been a lower level of technological and information support. This further compounds their educational handicaps. However, women with education have entered many new areas of occupation where their participation was virtually non-existent before. This process of occupational diversification through education has been accelerated during the Decade in many developing countries.

The enable women to participate actively in all spheres of economic and social life, vocational and professional training must be further developed. In this respect, the training of trainers is of primary importance, as is the introduction of management training for women. Apart from the conventional types of training (seminars, workshops, export group meetings training through doing, etc.), the non-conventional types are often also suitable. Of special relevance are also the new participatory types of training, which include learner-centered methods developed in the framework of non-formal education in which trainers are facilitators, to elicit productive response and interaction-and local social and cultural forms that can be built upon for effective training.

These include-decision making patterns, social groupings and communications networks. The major lacunae in educational development are in the areas of cultural change and promotion of social values which support and reflect the goals of development. Cultural transformations are taking place in developing countries, but in many cases through processes over which the people and even the governments have little control. New values and aspirations are often promoted, directly or indirectly, for profit maximisation-by forces inside or outside the country.

Changes in consumption patterns and role models are stimulated by mass media, commercial interests and a process of borrowing or emulation of life styles from developed countries. In many countries such changes have contributed to a widening of the gap between the elites and the masses of the people between the rural and urban populations, between the rich and the poor. This presents a challenge to the educational system, which must correct the trend if it is to promote the goals of participatory development, and collective self-reliance, eliminate the dependency on external support and contribute to comprehensive integrated development.

While there is evidence that the process of unplanned cultural change helps to promote illusory images which are far removed from the social realities of developing countries, cultural reaction, which tries to counter these influences by looking only to the past, may also have a negative impact on development. In their efforts to preserve their cultural identities developing countries have sought to reaffirm their attachment to their cultural heritage. While pride in this heritage can contribute to the spirit and the value of self-reliance, this process may also lead to distortions-to a withdrawal from present-day problems and realities to a glamorisation of the past, to the imposition of the culture of dominant groups on other culturally diverse groups and to a strengthening of some of the forces and institutions that oppose the goals of comprehensive, participatory development of all peoples, classes and groups.

Such trends have often inhibited the equality of women and attempts to enhance their role in development. Educational institutions will have to play an active role in the promotion of the development of such new cultural values. Hitherto, their contribution has been inadequate. Structurally pedagogically and philosophically, educational institutions will have to play a far more active role in the development of a new cultural context that can contribute to the realisation of the goals of comprehensive development—human and material.

This also requires that they internalise the concern for the equality of women and the enhancement of their role-in their curricula, pedagogic methods, organisation and research agendas. A strategic interrelationship between education and cultural and socio-economic development which integrates concern for the emancipation of women would have to be characterised by respect for the specific cultural features of a particular environment and clearly define the cultural and developmental function of education in social transformation and support the process of educational reform. Partically, in this connection, the promotion of new knowledge about women and new perceptions of the role of women in development could be viewed as an instrument for educational and cultural development with a view to:

(1) equal participation of the local population, and particularly of women, in devising, deciding upon and implementing development programmes; this can be acnieved by clearly defining the developmental interests of all groups of the population;

(2) strengthening and extension of training activities so as to embrace all relevant problems, such as: improvement of professional skills, education for family life and responsibilities, training for community organisation and management, decision waking etc.;

(3) promotion of integral and interdisciplinary links among developing countries in the field of cultural transformation and education and especially in professional and vocational training as well as in all forms of non- conventional training, to ensure availability of cadres capable of handling the new technology.

(4) enhancement of the collective self-reliance of nonaligned and other developing countries in culture and education by intensifying their communication in these fields, especially as regards the

methodologies for educational reform which incorporates the advancement of women as one of its concerns.

Role of Mass Media

Obviously, Communication media have been a powerful social influence, both as instruments of change and for maintaining *status quo.* In the last decade, an impressive amount of literature on the portrayal of women in the media has been produced.

These studies have expressed concern about the stereotyped and negative images of women which are being projected through the media without any cognizance of the new and expanded roles of women in society.

Communication media are a powerful tool for the creation of an alternative and positive image of women and could promote new attitudes and strategies for action directed towards the achievement of the goal of equality for women. It is imperative to democratises the control over the communication media and to make them an instrument for the creation of an awareness of women's needs and problems. Mass media, especially the audiovisual media, play an important role by influencing the consumption patterns and life-styles, and usually promote commercial interests (often of external producers), thus creating pressures to distort trade and industrial policies.

They also contribute to the distortion of cultural development, promoting imported values which militate against comprehensive integrated development and the principle of collective self-reliance. There has been a recent trend among media professionals in developing countries towards greater realism in their portrayal of social problems.

Realism, however, must be used to inspire people to struggle for change. A search for new options in human relationships, the reshaping of social institutions, political and economic structures and cultural values, would go a long way towards integrating women into the world of the media, and enable the media to play a more positive role in integrated development.

In the past, there has been a one-way flow of information from the developed to the developing countries, and from government to the people. The goals of self-reliance and participatory development, which are being actively pursued by the non-aligned countries, involve a shift from excessive reliance of the developing countries on foreign resources towards a mobilisation of their indigenous resources, which would make these countries less vulnerable to external pressures and develop their own potential for growth.

The new information and communication technology, the micro-chip revolution, has considerably magnified the power of the media. Satellite communication has exposed millions of people to new information. The strengthening of the autonomous capacities of the individual countries and improvement of the organisational framework and media content will depend on the socio-political context of each country. Women are today an important factor in the strategy of self-reliance and the media could do much to create public awareness of the role of women and their potentials. There are a number of steps which the media could take at various levels to strengthen the role of women as equal partners in development:

(1) horizontal communication and cooperation among developing countries in this field could be strengthened in order to create an awareness of

issues of common concern, identifying solutions to common problems and areas of cooperation.

(2) a democratisation of the structures and control of the communication media could contribute to the representation and participation of women in the media at the decision—making levels;

(3) more women should be involved in media training programmes; communication and advertising policies involving participation by women could be developed;

(4) media content could be improved through coordinated efforts for increased interaction between non-governmental organisations in formulating guidelines for monitoring programmes;

(5) listeners and viewers from consumer groups or NGO action groups, etc., could be effectively utilised to create an awareness of women's issues and to evolve common strategies for the promotion of more positive approaches to women's issues;

(6) various international seminars, conferences and expert group meetings, which have already covered a wide range of issues connected with women and the communication media indicate the need for further in depth studies, research training for women in communication technology, the organisational framework, including the development of a code of ethics with regard to the presentation of women in media and using traditional folk media to encourage participation of women.

The still largely unresolved problems of the interconnections between economic and social development and the increasing concern for the distributional and human dimensions of development indicate the need to pay more attention to all aspects of social development. The issues of health, social security, population trends and family planning, housing urbanisation and the environment, are linked with the general problem of the level of socio-economic development of a country its resource base and social policies.

Millions of people in developing countries are trapped in poverty, malnutrition, hunger and disease, although there are regional variations in living conditions. It is estimated that acute forms of potential energy malnutrition affect *35* per cent school children in Africa, 16 per cent in Asia and 4 per cent in of Latin America. Similarly, it is estimated that two-thirds pregnant women in the developing world suffer from nutritional anaemia. High maternal and infant mortality rates are closely linked with inadequate maternal and child health care services, lack of proper sanitation and a safe drinking water supply.

By the end of the last decade, only 42 per cent of households in developing countries had access to a potable water supply and over three quarters of the population lacked access to sanitary facilities. A disaggregation of social indicators by regions reveals that not only is there a very great gap between the developed and developing countries but also that there is great diversity among the developing regions. The average life expectancy in Sub-Saharan Africa is 47.4 years while it is 63.9 years in some Asian Countries. Similarly, infant mortality is highest in Sub-Saharan Africa (127.1 per thousand live births), while it is 56.2 in South East Asia.

In the South Asian region the mortality differentials by sex indicate higher infant mortality among females and empirical data also show sex-based health and nutrition related behaviour. In the health care sub-systems, there are interesting variations: Latin America—with the highest per capita GDP— has 7.5 physicians and 11.7 nurses per 10,000 population, followed by some countries in South East Asia, where despite low GDP per capita the averages are 5.4 physicians and 5.2 nurses per 10,000 population. In fact, most developing countries are faced with the problem of a decline or slowing down of the growth rate of production, rising unemployment, growing deficits in balance of payments and inflation.

All these adversely affect the availability of resources for social services, *i.e.*, health, education and social security. Despite the methodological weaknesses of the existing social indicators and an absence of data on access to and distributional characteristics of the social development infrastructure, the trends indicate that results differ sharply also within regions and that social improvements definitely do not come automatically as a by-product of economic growth. In many cases health resources are disproportionately concentrated in big cities, at the expense of primary health care for the masses in rural areas. Problems requiring careful study include disparities in increase and living standards, and the care available to different social groups, inadequate planning and management of health development, problems of inter and intra-sectoral coordination, administrative decentralisation and involvement of the people in the planning, programming and implementation of health care programmes. Very few developing countries have systems of social security. Even where such systems exist, a large part of the population in the informal sector—a substantial proportion of which are women—is not covered by the existing systems of mater benefits, health insurance, old age benefits, etc.

In some countries voluntary and philanthropic organisations supplement state action. However, their work is often uncoordinated and not adequate to deal with the increasing, demands of urbanisation and poverty. The development of social protection is linked to changes in the development strategies and orientation directed towards the satisfaction of basic minimum needs, the reduction and elimination of poverty, promotion of employment opportunities and improvement of the working conditions of labour. The global strategy of *Health for All by 2000* adopted by the Thirty Fourth World Health Assembly in 1981, which emphasises basic health protection, the primary health care approach and organisation of an effective health care and health information system, identified priorities for health cooperation and drew up an Action Programme, stressing the need for a review of a number of policy orientations in the areas of primary health care, health information and monitoring system, community involvement in health programmes, prevention of infectious diseases, development of national services of health care and health education, production, distribution and consumption of drugs and protection of the human environment. On the basis of the Medium-Term Programme for Technical Cooperation among Developing Countries for Health for All (1984-89) and in view of the calls for an acceleration of the development of national health care capabilities and the establishment of local points for TCDC in the area of health some priority activities may be identified: As the Mexico Conference on Population in 1984 stressed, population strategies cannot be limited to the analysis of population trends, since there is a dynamic interrelationship between these and socio-economic transformations. Hence, what is required is a set of coordinated strategies and activities for the promotion of economic development of the quality of life, human rights and in particular the fundamental right to individual choice.

The status of women and the advancement of their role in development remains a critical element in the achievement of these objectives. The persisting inequalities between men and women—which are evident in the higher incidence of poverty, unemployment and illiteracy among women—the limited range of employment categories offered to women, and the uneven sharing of borne and family responsibilities make it difficult for women to participate actively in the socio-economic development of the country. Population policies should be viewed as an integral part of overall socio-economic development. There is sufficient evidence to show that it is lower income groups with a low level of literacy, low and insecure income and low health and nutritional levels which have larger families. This is points to a need for planning policies which have a more integrated approach.

Rapid population growth will affect the efforts of countries to achieve food security and to reduce pressure on the natural resources; also, its effects on urbanisation and on land and capital will exacerbate inequalities. Many governments have launched subsidised family planning programmes. However, incentives are offered to encourage people to reduce family size.

Experience has shown that a clinical approach which threatens social values, beliefs and customs does not succeed and is actually a disincentive. To breakthrough the vicious circle of poverty, high fertility and mortality calls for a more careful and humane public policy with a judicious balance between individual choice and dignity and promotion of a sense of responsibility among parents to ensure a better future for all children.

This could be further stimulated and promoted through various forms of technical assistance at various levels as well as enriched through mutual exchange of information and experience among developing countries. The rapid growth of cities in developing countries has created serious problems, since a large proportion of urban migrant workers are living in temporary hutments and settlements without adequate basic amenities. The growth of cities and the steep rise in rural-urban migration is a manifestation of imbalances in the location and expansion of productive activity.

Women are particularly affected, as many of their activities are connected with their homes and bad housing and hygiene conditions are detrimental to both their own and their families health. The growth of cities has also created ecological problems. The growing demands of expanding cities have put undue pressure on natural resources, destroying the harmony between human beings and nature, and has led to a degradation of productive resources like water, land and forests. With increasing pressure on the land, overgrasing and deforestation, severe environmental damage has followed.

The expansion of agriculture by clearing large tracts of forest has caused desertification due to severe soil erosion, a problem which is extremely serious in Sub-Saharan Africa (Sahel), north-western Asia and the Middle East. Forests are crucial to the ecological life of many developing countries and deforestation has created serious problems, as the consumption of forest resources has exceeded replacement possibilities through natural growth. This has affected millions of rural households and the role of women in these households, as well as the nutritional level of the families. The human costs of malnutrition, famine and disruption in the lives of people seeking employment are a matter of serious concern. Environmental issues conceiving the environment in its broadest social context are most relevant for women.

The increasing marginalisation of certain sections of the population, growing poverty and deprivation of the masses, decreasing food production, the energy crisis and human environmental degradation in many developing countries are all symptoms of a pattern of growth and resource utilisation which is geared to existing power structures and prevents a large section of the population from satisfying its basic needs. The multidimensional problems facing developing countries are interconnected, but often these connection are not understood by those who formulate sectoral policies.

In the long run, social development policies will have to be closely integrated with economic development policies and a strong commitment to the improvement of the quality of life. The methods and instruments of analysis and planning of socio-economic development should therefore take adequate account of environmental constraint. Both the conceptual and sectoral parts of this study have indicated the basic features and tendencies of the changing role and status of women in developing countries. This was primarily the result of an analysis of the overall impact of development on the position of women in the societies of the developing countries and of the role of women in the developmental process. Basically, the effects of socio-economic development in individual sectors of the economy and public life have been identified and analysed.

The endeavours at operationalisation of national development policies, including the integration of women in development raised the issue of instruments and institutions to implement these policies. Issues addressed in this sections are: the role of government of public and private enterprises and of political participation and the role of women in decision-making processes as factors of development. In principle, most governments have accepted the improvement of the social, political, economic and legal status of women, and the integration of women into development as desirable goals and planning objectives. The response of government, parliament and other political institutions at various levels to the need for the integration of women's issues into development plans is important for the effective implementation of appropriate strategies.

Country experiences indicate that during the UN Decade for Women many countries established governmental machinery, either as part of the existing administrative structures, as independent agencies (commissions, bureaux, ministries) for women's affairs, or in the form of National Councils which were extra-governmental organisations. Most of these mechanisms were created with the objectives of establishing responsibility and accountability within the government for planning, programming and implementing programmes for women and to act as a catalyst; providing the necessary infrastructure and resource support and training personnel: and reviewing, monitoring and evaluating policies and programmes and their impact on women.

The Mid-Decade review of the efficacy of these administrative and institutional mechanisms indicated that the constraints to action have ranged from conceptual of resource and organisational fractional factors. They do not have strong executive and resource support and have a limited mandate. The tendency has been to locate such units mainly within departments of social welfare and culture which are considered non-productive and are usually not in the mainstream of the development effort and also suffer most from budgetary constraints during economic recession.

The experience of some developing countries also indicates that the existence of governmental or state mechanism of this kind tends to reduce the concern of other administrative organs and of society as a whole for the advancement of women and leads to a diminution of activity in this direction. As already indicated, the problems with regard to the role of women are closely linked with the problems of overall development.

However, most of the governments have perceived the role of women as a specific interest issue without making any attempt to integrate the problems involved into the mainstream of development planning. In many developing countries women—specific projects were designed to provide income—generating activities and basic needs to poor rural and urban women.

These efforts basically addressed the immediate needs for survival faced by women in the poorer sections, without addressing the multi-dimensional and multisectoral processes and structures that marginalise these women. The governmental bodies deliberating on the crucial strategies of food production, industrialisation rural development, science and technology, and monetary reforms still face the problems connected with the integration of the role of women into their overall plans of action.

It is becoming increasingly evident that issues related to the position of women cannot meaningfully be dealt with only through specific projects, without effectively linking them to economic policies, plans and programmes, and making these projects an integral part of the long-term process of development. The typical women and development projects may, however, perpetuate the reformist stance by promoting marginal, often non-viable activities not linked to major sectors of development and sometimes lead to a considerable increase in women's burden without providing the necessary supportive institutions for their new role and expanded opportunities.

They fail to deal with structural inequalities which lead to changes in policies and programmes and affect the allocative, distributive and participatory processes. The access of women to productive resources is a necessary precondition for their advancement. Recent discussions in both international and national flora have stressed issues such as title to land, access to credit and banking facilities, to employment on equal terms and under equal conditions, and to information and knowledge, education and training.

Any policy aimed at improving the lot of poorer households should involve substantial changes in resource control, e.g., land tenure, investment patterns, access to information regarding markets, technology, employment opportunities, availability of financial or other support, training etc., to increase women's control over their own labour and income. Answers to these issues will have to be found within the framework of nation states.

During the UN Decade for Women, besides the integrative approach, arguments for specific transitional strategies and policies by the government to deal with the historically disadvantaged position of women were put forward. The approach was based on the assumption that the understanding of the role of women could be strengthened within the complex framework of government by setting time-specific and measurable goals within each important sector, thus operationalising the concern for the position and role of women and translating it into programmes of action.

Further, recognising the close link between class and gender issues, it was expected that targetting for each group, in addition to the overall development target, would narrow the gender gaps in various sectors. To ensure a more meaningful intervention, a blending of the two approaches, i.e., integral development with specific action, is suggested. Minor transitional activities should be in line with the long-term perspectives, if they are not to be counter-productive. A survey conducted by the ILO in mid—1984, on the integration of the question of women in national development plans, reveals that only 12 of 44 developing countries has incorporated employment of women by sectors in their national development plans, 28 countries had set up governmental bodies dealing with the question of female workers, and only 19 of 44 countries had undertaken sectoral surveys to investigate the problems and prospects of female workers.

Much ground remains to be covered before the legal guarantees and administrative measures can be put into practice. Attempts at removing legal obstacles and improving access to education and other social services have not prevented growing poverty and malnutrition, rising unemployment and underemployment coupled with an increasing work burden, and persistent marginalisation of women in the economy and in decision-making structures, although there have been varying results in the individual countries and regions. However, governments have experienced considerable difficulties in their attempts to articulate these new approaches in policies and development action.

These are due to a number of factors: the persistent

invisibility of women as a critical and important factor within development structures; continued lack of awareness and understanding of the difficulties that women face even when they are participating on equal terms in development—both as beneficiaries and as agents; and delays in developing an adequate set of monitoring and evaluation measures and instruments to speed up effective implementation of adopted policies.

The most urgent task which now faces governments is more innovative blending of the role of women into the design of action programmes, policy instruments and evaluation criteria or monitoring procedures in all sectors of development. The issue of women's role in development cannot be a concern of women only. The value-creating mechanisms, i.e., the educational system, and the media, may be suitably modified to project values of sex equality.

Governments could modify or eliminate legal provisions that still uphold the unequal status of women. The strategies for action suggested in the sectoral chapters all call for operational instruments. Who is to initiate, implement and evaluate these measures at the national and at the regional and international levels? The emphasis should be on perceptional, organisational and infrastructural development.

At the government level, executive and administrative measures need to be taken to ensure recognition of women's productive, reproductive and participatory roles and to provide supportive services such as child care and need social services, i.e., health care, education, catering, housing and drinking water, etc., to reduce their work burden and enable them to assume wider responsibilities. What kind of policy instruments have been effective in incorporating the role of women into sectoral structures? A concerted effort is needed to bridge the gap between the highest levels of government and the intermediate and lower levels where plans are operationalised. A comparison of organisational and infrastructural models and approaches in different countries could provide an insight into the strengths and weaknesses of various arrangement.

The Mexico Conference had visualised the National Commission as watchdog bodies—to review and recommend measures necessary to enhance the equality and participation of women in development and decision making. Some countries have defined the functions of the national mechanisms in this manner and provided them with the requisite powers of resource support. At the same time the strength of the argument that women's affairs cannot be separated from the sectoral agencies responsible for planning and implementation of development in the fields of agriculture and rural development, industry, energy, science and technology, urban and rural development, education, health and other social services must be acknowledged.

Since the objective is the integration of women in all these sectors of development, it could be useful to institutionalise this concern, or mandate—to continue the task of making the Sectoral agencies sensitive, concerned and accountable. Such sectoral mechanisms could also continue to increase the level of competence of women, advancing their role in development in various sectors.

In view of the stagnation of overall development, the modest resource support has kept efforts to promote the role of women at a marginal level in most developing countries. Thus in some developing countries such efforts have been primarily dependent on international aid.

Apart from the fact that this may have precluded the

integration of these efforts into major development sectors, this dependence has in some cases also diverted attention from the goals of collective and national self-reliance, and sometimes also distorted national priorities. The incorporation of the aspects of the role of women in development in existing teaching/training and research institutions may reduce investments in physical and administrative infrastructure—and improve the prospects for integrating/articulating women's problems, issues and concerns within all educational institution/disciplines, instead of allowing them to remain a separate, marginal activity, whose isolation makes it ineffective.

National, regional and international networks of such institutions should be encouraged to share and expand share and expand their experiences, which would help to increase their competence, and strengthen the ties or intellectual and developmental co-operation among non-aligned nations. Such efforts would help to increase the extent and improve the quality of data needed by national governments.

They would also make it possible to train an increasing number of cadres to take up the various functions identified as necessary for the advancement of women in development. Above all, the incorporation of studies of this kind within the educational systems and in training institutions would help promote the needed cultural, transformation.

Science and technology, which could be powerful instruments for the advancement of the role of women in development have so for usually by-passed women because their educational and other handicaps. Science and technology have also often been misused to marginalise women and reduce their status. It is therefore important not merely to facilitate the access of women to science and technology, but also to ensure that practitioners will be aware of the problems involved in the employment of women in his areas.

It would be useful to introduce these concerns as early as the training stage. In particular, developments in the fields of communication technology and communication sciences pose a critical challenge to the decisions of the non-aligned Countries to enhance the role of women in development. If these new developments are not harnessed in accordance with the policies for the advancement of women, they will continue to be used by social forces which oppose the equality of women and development, and help to strengthen and perpetuate values and behavioural norms that thrive on the subordination of women.

The transfer of technology in some of these fields has already bad consequences which militate against the improvement of the status of women. The improvement of the systems for data collection and development of quantitative and indicators for measuring women's development is another critical area.

Despite repeated decisions at various international conferences, many national data collection agencies still do not have adequate data on women, nor do they provide sex break-downs or gender differentiation in different fields. They continue to be pervaded with a biased understanding of what is important information regarding the status of women and its impact on the conditions and equality of life of families, communities and development in general. Similarly, there has been little follow-up action at the national levels to the very useful international efforts and decision to develop and compile comparable socioeconomic indicators to measure the role of women in development, as initiated recently by INSTRAW and the UN Statistical Office.

A system of reporting by sex disaggregated data would help the flow of information from the bottom up, monitoring the actual implementation of programmes and benefits accuring to women, and through women to the entire community, and increase the accountability of government agencies. Simultaneously, such a process would initiate improvement of data systems, concepts and methods of statistics, and development of indicators. Numerous studies from developing countries have demonstrated the importance of women's grass-root participatory organisations.

When genuinely participatory they become dynamic instruments—not merely for the advancement of women, but for the improvement of the quality of the development process as a whole. But in many developing countries; such organisations have not yet been evolved. Where women's cooperatives, village level organisations and voluntary agencies to exist, they generally receive little support in the way of resources, information or recognition.

In some cases, the efforts of non-governmental organisation have provided some support to break the isolation of these grass-root groups. The NGOs have often played the role of an intermediary, providing the needed support to the grass-root groups helping to establish direct communications between them and development agencies, and also helping to develop networks of grass-root groups to enable them to learn from each other.

An important strategy for governments to consider is recognition of some organisation/institutions as intermediaries to increase the governments' reach, to obtain the needed feed-back from the grass roots and to raise the level of information and knowledge at both ends. The concept of intermediaries provides a new channel for organisation/ institutions outside the government to play a role in advancing the status of women in development and help operationalise some of the strategies already accepted. The concept of an autonomous intermediary— supported by government resources and acting as a channel of communication between grass-root groups and government without the negative features of a patron-client relationship at either end.

Strategies

It is pertinent here to suggest strategies to further strengthen the role of women in the overall development efforts could be oriented towards:

1. continuation and redoubling of efforts to make the role of women visible in various sectors of development, in various agencies and instruments for government action, such as the legislature, the judiciary, planning agencies. public enterprises, specialised agencies created by governments for particular aspects of economic and social development, financial institutions, etc.;
2. reviewing, monitoring and evaluating policies and programmes and their impact on women in development and *vice versa* —from an integrated and coordinated point of view;
3. provision of the necessary infrastructure, resource and cadre support for planning and execution of the governmental policies in this regard;
4. promotion of value transformation, in view of the long-term objective of the advancement of the role of women in development;

5. further research and training of all those involved and concerned in promoting the status of women information gathering systems should be promoted in order to provide essential inputs for government policies and actions;
6. enhancement of the opportunities for women to take part in decision making as fully informed citizens;
7. access of women as well as of men, to information on the decisions taken by their governments, on available assistance and support and agencies and structures from which to obtain such support;
8. raising of the literacy level and upgrading and dissemination of knowledge. This is where communication technology and traditional communication channels should be harnessed;
9. exchange of information and experience, as well as consultative arrangements at venous levels, particularly at the regional and inter-government levels. In this matter a number of international, regional or interregional institutions might be requested to assist the identification of communication channels;
10. elaboration of guidelines for all bilateral and multilateral technical cooperation programmes to ensure the incorporation of elevant aspects of the role of women in development. The UNDP Indicative Planning Figure should also incorporate these aspects for basic programmatic action;
11. inclusion of the question of the role of women in development in the preparation of plans for negotiations at all stages of the project cycle at

different levels of regional and international cooperation, so as to ensure that the result of these projects will not be in conflict with national objectives;

12. incorporation of a social impact analysis into all projects to avoid negative results. Non-aligned countries' cooperation could help to develop the necessary methodology for such analyses;
13. continuation of the work already initiated by national and international research institutions in refining and building up an adequate analysis (conceptual and methodological) and identification of indicators which can measure the work done by women, especially in food production and agriculture.

Data time series data should reflect the real position of women within the context of overall long-term trends in development. Research should include gender-specific analysis to illustrate the types of inequality which still require measures to overcome them.

Entrepreneurship Application

Remarkably, one of the important factors in the development programmes and plans of developing countries is the growth and expansion of public enterprises and the public sector. Initially, public enterprises operated principally in the infrastructure and the public utilities, but their range of activity has now considerably expanded. Being part of the broader stream of the public sector in developing countries, public enterprises are important instruments of national and collective self-reliance and are oriented towards increasing the countries autonomy in using and developing their natural and human resources in order to increase the well-being of the population as a whole.

One of the responsibilities of public enterprises is the promotion of the integration of women into the developmental process and of a conscious policy directed towards the advancement of women. The responsibilities of public enterprises in this regard, however, differ in accordance with their scope and nature, their mandate and function, their scope and coverage of national planning and the legislative framework. But, by and large, they cover a wide range of commercial and; or non-commercial functions of great importance in everyday life.

Practical experience in the operation of public interprises in developing countries has shown that they generate progressive social change in these countries, including positive moves towards involving women in the main streams of development. However, the public sector in general and the public enterprises in particular are still not strong enough to constitute a major or even a very important factor in involving women in the transformation of their socio-economic position and are thus not making a sufficient response to this complex task.

Within the framework of the national development programmes, the public enterprise in general, and each specific enterprise in particular should be provided with guidelines indicating the special steps expected from the enterprise for the promotion of the role of women in developing countries.

These can include:

(1) More emphasis on clarity of aims and objectives, a regular review of the current status of women, including job profiles for the improvement of the position of women in training programmes, social welfare measures relating to child bearing and child

rearing, provision of creches and the allocation of specific responsibilities to appropriate national institutions;

(2) identification of areas of activity in which women are currently not represented but can be recruited. The human resources development plans should include a specific component on the employment of women;

(3) preparation of concrete action plans which should include both short-term and long-term strategies in the area of manpower planning, recruitment systems promotional opportunities, incentives, training and women's representation at the management level. These strategies should also envisage a regular procedure and criteria for the evaluation of the performance of public enterprises in terms of the fulfilment of economic and social objectives;

(4) in view of the need to involve more women at higher levels of management, special training programmes for the induction of women at these levels of enterprise management could be stimulated and developed as a short-term measure;

(5) efforts should be made to involve more women in on going training courses, particularly management training, as well as to develop the curricula of these courses with an emphasis on the role and responsibilities of public enterprises in the advancement of women;

(6) public enterprises should exploit their opportunities of generating employment in down-stream activities with which they are related. This is of particular

significance in the case of sub-contracting to public sector ancillaries. Some cases of sub-contracting to women's cooperatives and to regional development corporations which stimulate small business could also promote both employment and entrepreneurship among women. However steps must be taken to ensure that such practices are not deterimental to the position of women or to the overall regional development;

(7) Fuller involvement of women workers and men workers alike in decision-making processes as well as in forms of management at all levels of enterprise organisation, which is seen as an essential means of their advancement, parallel with the improvement of public enterprises' management patterns and efficiency;

(8) an agreed system of performance evaluation arising from the predetermined corporate plans should identify the evaluation criteria for each social objective including the objective of advancing the status of women. Whenever possible, an attempt should be made to quantify the criteria;

(9) the existing or/and newly created mechanisms at the national level responsible for scrutinising the policies and practice of public enterprises and evaluating their operations and contributions towards the socio-economic objectives of development could advise governments on the formulation of policies through which public enterprises could act as model employers and real promoters of the status of women, and could also undertake regular evaluation and monitoring of these efforts of public enterprises.

Apart from these, governments should seek appropriate ways and means to ensure that public and private enterprises share the responsibilities for the improvement of the status of women.

Some suggestions in this connections might be:

(1) private enterprises are established in developing countries under various systems of public licensing which include certain provisions for the enforcement of laws and these could be used for regulating the working conditions of women;

(2) it may expected that the linkages between the public and private enterprises could promote the realisation of some of these ideas.

(3) similarly, credit/banking agencies which give loans to private enterprises for equity and working capital could give specific incentives for the promotion of the advancement of women;

Remarkably, the political status of women in developing countries and the levels and quality of their political participation, are far from adequate, considering their share in the population structure, their part in social and economic reproduction, as well as their actual and potential role in the national development process. The unfavourable economic and social position of women in developing countries is directly reflected in the level of their participation in decision-making process at all levels.

In many developing countries a large portion of the women actively participated in the national liberation movements and in the creation of national political structures. However, they were often under-represented in the decision-making processes, in public and political life. Studies on women's participation have revealed that they are more active at the informal levels, which are closer to their problems than in formal political activity. This passivity of women in formal political activity is both a symptom and a cause of some major developmental problems. The political participation of women has always been indicative of their position in general. Today, there are only very few developing countries where national law excludes women from formal political processes. However data on a global basis indicate an enormous disparity between women's formal political equality and their actual participation in decision-making processes. Having understood this problem and recognised it as an important barrier to social and economic progress and development changes, most developing countries have been adopting and trying to implement policies and measures which would mitigate and remove it. Many of these efforts and measures have been promoted through the implementation of UN instruments, such as the Convention on Equal Political Rights of Women, the Convention on the Elimination of All Forms of Discrimination Against Women, etc.

There has been general recognition among those in authority in developing countries of the great importance of women's participation in the efforts towards social and human welfare.

A general summary of the findings of numerous studies in this field shows that the number of women who actively realise their role in development and their rights in developing countries is continuously increasing, as is the importance of their participation in representative and legislative for at the national, regional and particularly at the local level.

Women are especially active and are gaining increasing representation in local self-government bodies. The number of women in executive orans, in the judiciary, and in particular among high officials and in the political structures and public services is small and inadequate, but nevertheless growing. Their representation in the upper management echelons in the economic, scientific, cultural and social fields is unsatisfactory, but it cannot be said that the situation is not improving. In some regions political education and economic emancipation of women, as well as the creation of better family and household conditions have led to increased participation of women in political parties, trade unions, various movements, etc..The need for effective and extensive popular participation, promotion of grass-root organisations and institutional mechanisms to facilitate such participation has already been recognised. There will have to be a commitment from governments to provide opportunities for greater participation of women in political and other fields of life and to eliminate all forms of discrimination.

Examples of decentralised planning and decision-making, such as community development programmes, may be seen as positive moves towards the realisation of such commitments. In many developing countries genuine forms of popular participation have been established and are operating successfully, workers participation in management, industrial democracy, co-determination, self-management, etc.

Most of these relate to the sphere of the economy, the public sector and public enterprises, but are often accompanied by various forms of citizens involvement in running the community's affairs at the local and regional levels. Workers and citizens involvement in the conduct of economic and community affairs also includes forms of direct sharing in the management of public and social services, cooperative, consumers associations, etc. All these forms, which have given women art opportunity to enlarge the scope of their participation in public and political life, have had a significant impact on the overall activisation of women in society in the mainstream of development processes.

Such forms and experiences of workers, citizens and generally popular participation involving women equally, generate development and contribute to the realisation of human rights. This is being recognised by many international and UN fora and documents and should be fully considered by the development countries in applying strategies for the advancement of women. Taking into account the overall context—constrained national economies, inequalities in societies and the high barriers to greater participation of women in political life—an organisational base is crucial for the promotion of a more dynamic role for women in the process of development. However, a supportive infrastructure (government, the academic system, education the media, etc.), is often also important.

Non-governmental organisations—ranging from international to national and grass-root level organisations—have a long history of fighting for political rights for women, campaigning for changes in laws and national policies and participating in democratic and civil rights movements peace movements and ecological movements. The UN Decade for Women witnessed a reactivisation of women's organisations and the emergence of new women's groups with an increasing emphasis on collective action for articulating women's concerns and increasing women's visibility to development planners and decision makers.

There is a decisive shift now from social welfare work to involvement in income-generating projects, consumer rights and workers' right issues.

The Decade also saw the emergence of radical action groups protesting against sex violence against women and curbs on women's liberties and rights. Self-help action groups have also emerged at the grass-root level to articulate women's employment needs and increase their access to credit, developmental inputs and services. The importance of the role of non-governmental organisations lies particularly in their function as mobilising mechanisms and organising agencies of working women, protecting their interests, particularly in the informal sectors and providing necessary support services.

Further they act as mediators between government and the people and between coordinating agencies for the provision developmental inputs and services, as well as pressure groups and catalysts for the development of cadres and local leadership potential and organisational skills. However, in surplus labour economies and in economies in which women are largely employed in the informal sectors, it has proved extremely difficult to set up such organisations. In the organised sector, even where women are members of the trade unions they do not exercise authority within them because of their low position in the occupational hierarchy and they are by and large excluded from collective negotiation with employers. Female membership in trade unions is low, since there are no pressure on unions alter their priorities. In some countries, trade unions have created women's wings to specifically articulate the need of women workers.

There are also examples of separate women's trade

unions, workers organisations, particularly of women workers in the informal sectors of the economy who remain outside the purview of small producers is a must, but supportive structures are equally essential for survival of such organisations. There is a school of thought which maintains that separate women's organisations only divide the workers' movements. And in some cases such organisations neither succeeded in involving more women in public and political life nor did they gain social support.

8

Womanpower—The Neglected Factor in Development

"Business and labour are different sides of the same problem. It is impassible wisely to treat either without reference to the interests and duties of the other--and without reference to the fact that interests of the general public, the commonwealth, are paramount to both."

—***Theodore Roosevelt***

Introduction

Womenpower constitutes the half of the manpower. But neglect of womanpower in our society in perhaps the most important cause of our backwardness. Nearly 82 per cent of our women are illiterate and most of them live in the remote part of the country; they are not even aware of the rights to which they are entitled. Thus, they do not demand the enforcement of their rights within the family, community or nation. Countries that hope to be in the vanguard of economic development and social change should accord woman as high a status as that of man to enable both the sexes to play the necessarily complementary role in the progress of the nation. Ancient India was on the top of world map because the fair sex worked shoulder to shoulder with their counterpart and participated in all aspects of national life.

Though there is no dearth of talent among half of our population even today, they have been constantly denied the right to take active part in the mainstream of national development especially in the labour market.

No country has developed rapidly over a long period without having been to some extent liberating women from their traditional household chores and without their close association in various socio-economic productive oriented programmes. Only a few of the women have left the sheltered and protected life of home and managed to venture into the wider world. A literate and working woman cannot only minimise the wasteful expenditure on marriages and population growth but also plan the family budget and nutrition in a better way.

She can break the barriers of superstition and evil customs and help create a new society where womenpower play a vital role. Though women constitute half of our population without proper education and training they can hardly become partners in the developments around them. Education to a woman means educating the whole family. This will result in eradication of poverty as well as removal of inequalities between men and women. A woman's capability for leadership is obviously nurtured through her dealings with many household members under her command and control.

But only an educated or a working woman can contribute substantially to the national development. The role of woman in our society even as career woman not to speak of that as housewife is not insignificant.

WOMENPOWER AND RELEVANT ISSUES

They have achieved reputation as active politicians, efficient administrators and good jurists. Their contribution to scientific research and armed forces is also noteworthy. They have played a significant role in the socio-economic and political development of our country. The old order which confined women to the home as servants helpers to their menfolk, has been or is in the process of being replaced by a new one in which women increasingly undertake to fulfil many roles, within the home, as wives, mothers and home makers, and outside it, as partners and coworkers of men in all types of enterprises. According to 1971 Census women working on top jobs were: 2500 Engineers and Technicians; 300 Aircraft and Ships Officers, 100 Life Scientists; 23000 Physicians and Surgeons; 100 Economists and Related Workers; 16000 Social Scientists and Related Workers; 1700 Jurists, 500 Legislative Officers; 5300 Working Proprietors, Directors and Managers and Auditors and 3000 Village Officers. It shows that women are taking up jobs which were hitherto a male preserve.

A hierarchical order assigning least qualified jobs for women, while nearly all more qualified jobs and the supervisory jobs were meant for men is now being broken. It is, however, unfortunate that the socio-economic and legal reforms towards the uplift of women have awakened only a few of them about their rights and duties. The few fortunate women who have had the benefits of higher education seems to be quite oblivious of their immense responsibilities for the emancipation of the millions of women in the country-side and of the working and middle class families in urban areas.

Also for many among these educated women, education seems to be just a luxurious pastime.

Career for the Few

A majority of the women are at a disadvantage in

gaining admittance to professional training because of unequal access to education at preparatory levels. This affected their chances for admission to both academic and on-the-job training programmes. The disproportionately small number of women in craftsmen training is the obvious reason.

One reason why women of India re not marching ahead with confidence and taking their due place on the social and economic life of the nation is that only very few women job-seekers had obtained their professional competency because of prevailing social prejudices against women's higher education and lack of training facilities, consequently the interest of the well-being of women has been neglected.

Training of women as engineers and technicians is also grossly neglected. With such a large number of women deprived of career jobs we have failed in creating a just and equitable society. Productive capacity of women can be raised by making available to them the facilities for vocational education and training.

Women in White-Collar Jobs

Remarkably, in both the industrially advanced and less developed countries, women are burdened with cumulative inequalities as a result of socio-cultural and economic discriminatory practices which, until recently, have been taken for granted as though they were a part of the immmutable scheme of things established by nature. In the developing countries, as elsewhere, the comparative low level of women's wages indicates that women are concentrated in jobs and occupations low in the scale of skill and wages. (United Nations, 1974, p. 246).

All over the world women are denied equal access with men to opportunities for personal growth and social development in education, employment, marriage and family, professional and political life. In India as in the developed countries, women as less likely than men to continue their education to higher levels and are more likely to be found concentrated in females occupations like teaching, nursing, social work, typing and stenography—all of which have low status and low remuneration.

Even those women who have surmounted the hurdles to professional education are disadvantaged as women because of the difficulty of reconciling the competing and often incompatible home-making responsibilities. According to one estimate near about three fourths of the educated women are working as clerks, despatchers, typists, office assistants and receptionists. Out of 9.18 lakhs of women work-seekers registered with the employment exchange at the end of 1973, as many as 69,355 were seeking clerical and related jobs. The situation is somewhat good now as in 2010.

It is remarkable that the largest numbers of female workers are concentrated in Class III, i.e., ministerial and related staff. Giving reasons why women were unable to work in responsible posts Hate says, "Administrative high level work and business aptitude require sole and life-long attention to and ambition in the enterprise, one or more in hand, like an inventor or scientist. Besides wide contacts, quick decisions and extensive information are necessary.

Women, naturally and traditionally bound down to home, is so far found unable to fulfil this role, much more as her attention is half divided between the demands of the family and outside work." (Hate, 1969). There are several reasons why this pattern of occupational segregation and the exclusion of women from positions of executive authority and leadership are maintained.

First, socialisation in the family and education in the school reinforce 'gender roles', i.e., cultural definitions of the tradition—its and behaviour that are considered appropriate for men and women (Krauss, 1974). In school, girls are encouraged to aspire to a limited range of occupations which are believed to be 'feminine' and compatible with the demands of their primary gender roles of housewife and mother. Second, women lack role models in the scientific and technical occupations, in management, politics and public administration.

The few who are in these fields, have very little impact on the society as a whole. Third, it has been suggested that women, as a subordinate group in society, have internalised 'self-sacrificing and expressive' values and developed a 'false consciousness' which includes beliefs in the appropriateness of lower pay, of doing manual work, and of eschewing leadership positions and politics. Thus women are expected to seek occupational roles which stress the aspect of service and cooperation with men, not competition. Bernard notes that "when occupational sacrifices have to be made, the wife is usually happy to be the one to make them, subordinating her own career to that of her husband's" (1957, p. 350). Socioeconomic and politico-cultural changes in the life of women would help them as well as society in its development. In all occupations, men far outnumbered women and this is true even of ministerial work where workers are concentrated. Some of the occupations are fully male.

Though the proportion of man to women has come down during the two censuses the jobs still remain predominantly male. It may be noted that the definitions of workers in two censuses are different. But whatever definition, we adopt there is a very wide gap between the numbers of men and women employed. Women generally, have no scope for improving their earning capacity and thus continue to stagnate in their present jobs. The chances of their promotion is generally blocked particularly in private sector as the employers still have a general but wrong suspicion about their performance in higher posts.

Growing Unemployment

No developing society like ours should ignore the vast educated unemployment as it is a wastage of money and manpower. Nearly one crore people are already on the registers of employment exchanges and every 50 to 60 lakhs able-bodied people sought entry in the employment market. Of them, the position of women-job-seekers.

Remarkably, women are the greatest victims of technological unemployment brought about by the rapid increase in the modern and organised sector of industry as the processes of production are being transferred reducing the demand for unskilled labour. The incidence of seasonal unemployment is also higher among women and this will be shown subsequently.

Generally speaking, women are employed in the unsophisticated unskilled and low wage sector, mostly in monotonous, repetitive jobs or down-right menial tasks. The 1971 census reported 31 million female workers out of a population of 264 million females in the country. The workers were predominantly rural (28 million) only 3 million being from urban areas. The largest proportion (22.68%) of the female workers in rural areas belonged to the age-group 30-39, followed by the age-group 40-49 (16.71%) while 9.6 per cent of the female workers were under 15 years of age, 5.32 per cent were still working after the age of 60. According to 1971 census, the overall work-force participating rate for females is 13.1 per cent for rural and 6.6 per cent for urban areas. The corresponding figures for males are 53.5 per cent and 48.8 per cent.

Though women had played distinctive and accepted roles in the process of production and exchange in the traditional economy, as cultivators, artisans, traders, and professionals, revolution has resulted in a decline in women's participation.

During this decade the male and female population increased by 25 per cent and 24 per cent respectively, the number of male workers increased by 15.2 per cent while that of women declined by 41.2 per cent. The employment position of women in other sectors of the economy is equally heart breaking. In 1971 women engaged in trade and commerce was 0.5 million, inspite of the fact that in the metropolitan cities semiliterate women of the middle class had entered shops and commercial establishments in search of new avenues of employment. Women hardly comprise 4 per cent of the total labour force in textile industry and not more than 5 per cent in hosiery and knitting mills.

As such if we just examine women workers in terms of their education level we find that the most striking fact about rural and urban areas is that those women having education beyond middle school constitute barely 1 per cent of the total women employed in all sectors. In all these sectors of the economy women continue to be concentrated in a limited number of occupations and mostly at relatively low levels of skill and responsibility. (see Table 13.5)

Women have been and are being discriminated against in the matter of providing them with productive employment and are comensurate wages for their work. Wages and earnings of women lag far behind those of men generally speaking in industry and even more in agriculture.

The continuation of a stable system of occupational segregation is clearly related to the fact that women working full time and year-round earn about 50 to 70 per cent of male earnings for the same job. Women earn less than man because: (a) they are relegated to low paying job; (b) they are clustered in low paying occupations as they experience a higher rate of skill atrophy as a function of their intermittent labour force participation; (c) they are working in selective occupations inflating the labour supply for those occupations; (d) differences in male and female rates of return for investments in human capital account for a large part of the earnings differential; (e) differential earnings between males and females are also due to their education, experience, hours worked and occupational prestige.

Lack of women in organising themselves into strong trade unions is also one of the most important reasons for their exploitation. Though the male female differentials in earnings may be explained by the above objective factors, yet one cannot rule out discrimination against female labour which must cause concern to all those who are interested in improving their social and economic position.

Besides giving to the women special social protection, it is the duty of society not to deny to them equal pay for equal work. It seems that laws are on women's side but prejudice, hostilities and resistence still hold them back. In order to usher in for all a better and brigher era women worker's interest in our society must be safeguarded not by promises but by actual deeds. A lot of human power is wasted at home remaining idle without work and used for production only seasonally. If we just examine some statistic on the social life of rural population regarding the time they spend outside the labour force, we will find that most of this human power is wasted as they have no productive work to attend.

The total duration of wage employment has registered a downward trend for both the sexes, both in agricultural and all rural labour households. Unfortunately, we have miserably failed to recognise this vast potential resources, we have in our rural population. We must make every effort to harness the total availability of our national humanpower to creative and productive purposes.

This is possible only if we change from technological oriented economy to cottage-based industry. Then alone women would be able to joint the workforce and thus help to increase the per capital income, while at the same time helping to bring up the future generation of young men and women adequately prepared to take their places in the technologically and socially advanced society of the day.

It is unfortunate that the work done at home by woman is regarded as unremunerative. Our Economists and Satisticians are to be blamed for this as they have deliberately omitted their supposedly non-productive labour from national accounts statistics, even though it has been estimated that the invisible work of housewives in fact represents some 25-40 per cent of GLP (Clark, 1958, p. 204-ii). If at all her services are needed outside home under economic pressure and to play a constructive role in society it is equally important that her counter part must share some domestic burden.

However, in practical life it has been seen that an

average working wife is expected to return home to take care of the children, to cook, tidy up the house, launder and iron the clothes, doing minor stiching, repair her children's stocks and get their school work done to that they may be well equipped to fact the world next morning. An educated husband on the other hand has freedom to visit libraries, attend talks, discussions and seminars and in general pursue his academic interests without a thought to the drudgery his wife has to return to. While welcoming his wife's earnings, the Indian male refuses in his selfishness to share even a fragment of the domestic routine.

What is needed today is to give recognition to the social nature of women's work in the family by way of housework and child care. Only by providing socially arranged services for these activities women will be able to play an equal part in the development of our society. What has gone wrong, in the field of employment of women in jobs which till now were the preserve of men is that we have put the cart before the horse. It is like expecting an underdeveloped economy to take off towards growth by putting up heavy industry and forgetting that there is something far more important called the infrastructure.

In the same way we have launched women into working in a life big way without cultivating the proper culture for it, without preparing society for accepting such a noval move with an open mind. To improve this situation we shall have to reform society radically by changing the respective roles played by men and women, in the family, in productive and non-productive work, in the management of the economy and public affairs, and above all in people's minds. Let us create such an infrastructure first and then expect their greater involvement in working force.

Unless such a corresponding change occurs in the role

and relative expectations on both sides, it is difficult, if not impossible, for an average women to go up the professional ladder.

Health and Family Planning

It is pertinent to note that three major goals of the population control measures are: (i) improved quality of life, (ii) improved economic wellbeing, and (iii) survival itself. The women, whose health and life is constantly endangered due to inadequate diet, over work in home and in occupation if employed, frequent child-bearing and rearing etc. are also badly neglected when it comes to their illness.

Women are seldom given the same medical treatment as given to men when they are sick. As a result of this callous attitude, which still persists in many parts of the country, the incidence and duration of sickness is more pronounced in the case of women. Giving reasons for this Mazumdar writes, "their increasing displacement from the economic process is the main cause of the high level of malnutrition and mortality among women and children" (1976, p. 17).

The death rate among child-bearing women is 8-10 times higher in India than that in developed nations. An Indian woman from a poor socio-economic group gains only a round 4-6 kgs, during pregnancy while the Western woman puts on upto 12 kgs. Since most of our women suffer from various vitamin and mineral deficiencies, the mother's health is adversely affected.

A net result of this malnutrition of mothers is that most babies born in India weigh only about 2.6 kgs. as against the weighs of 3.4 kgs. of a normal baby. If women are assured of their health and longer life of their children they will surely favour smaller families.

Current Demographic Trends

Currently the age of marriage of boys and girls has been raised to 21 and 18 years respectively. The purpose of fixing the minimum age of marriage of females is to combat two evils: (a) to prevent the evils of permature child-birth and death, and (b) to increase the expectation of life so that the couples may be persuaded to accept contraceptives. These objectives have been achieved to some extent but there has not been any significant effect on the growth of population as our population is still increasing at the rate of 2.4 per cent with the result that women are constantly becoming weaker and weaker. Hence there is an urgent need to adopt family planning in a big way.

Thus, no one can afford to ignore that various programmes directly connected with the women's health and welfare if their active participation in the family planning programme as well as the main stream of national development is to be sought.

Education

Though there is a tremendous increase during post-independence period in the number of school and college going girls, it falls too short of that of boys. It was estimated that in 1976-77 girls enrolled in Classes I-V constituted only 67.1 per cent of the relevant age-group whereas boys constituted 102.0 per cent. The disparity increases as we compare the enrolment of girls and boys at successively higher stages. Girls in Classes VI-VIII constituted 24.8 per cent of the relevant age-group whereas boys figures were 49.9 per cent. In 1974-75 the number of girls enrolled in IX-XI Classes were 26,42,580 (10.9%) against 65,01,143 (26.2%) for boys. Enrolment figures for girls in higher education are even more discouraging. There were 8,50,767 girls (2.5%) at college standard as against 22,27,036 (6.2%) boys.

The existing gap between the education of men and women need to be narrowed so that the gains of education to the fair sex in all the stages may reach them. This is possible if special measures like starting separate educational institutions for girls are undertaken particularly in these areas where social prejudices inhibit enrolment of girls in co-education and the recruitment of female teachers at all levels are pressed for vigorously. Among other programmes need to be taken up for the benefit of women are non-formal education, general education accompanied by vocational education condensed-course particularly for growing women.

It is well-known that dropout rate is very high in Classes I-V. In 1976-77, it is estimated that for every 100 children that enter Class I, only about 40 complete Class V and about 25 complete Class VIII. It is a fact that dropout rate in the case of girls from rural areas and from the less privileged section of the society is as heavy as 42.85 per cent between Classes I and II. The hard core of non-enrolled children are girls, particularly in the rural areas and children belonging the Scheduled Castes. Scheduled Tribes, Landless Agricultural Labourers and Urban Slum Dewellers. The difference between the rates of wastage and stagnation for boys (66.3%) and girls (71.36%) is quite substantial. It is 42.85 per cent between grades I and II, 12.2 per cent between grades III and IV and 8 per cent between grades IV and V.

While the economic and educational reasons of wastage and stagnation applied to a large extent both to boys and girls, in the case of girls, social factors like early marriage, betrothal, family chores, social prejudices in rural areas and parental apathy to girl's education play a more significant part. This adversely affects not only the overall progress of women's education but their career as well. Educational programme should, therefore, be so designed as to bring down the rate of dropout among girls-students.

In spite of much socio-economic and political progress life still remain difficult for a woman than a man.

The mere granting of the political vote to women or any other forms of legal equality would be of little purpose. Some legislations have already been enacted for the benefit of working women. The remuneration Act, though welcome, covers only women employed in factories, tea, coffee and cashew plantations. It does not cover women engaged in construction and agriculture. The most deplorable and miserable conditions of village women particularly of those belonging to backward classes and those living in slums of big towns cannot be overlooked. In all attempts to rehabilitate and to safeguard the basic economic security India's teaming millions from their subsistence level women folk cannot be ignored. Besides material comforts, intellectual and moral growth is essential for any worth living. In planning socio-economic prosperity, mineral and other natural resources should not monopolise all attention and effort.

The most valuable capital of India lies dorment in her educated and uneducated unemployment and educational psychological planning of this human riches is indispensable if social welfare is to be maximised. Women do not live in vacuum. She is part and parcel of society. It is to the advantageous of the society itself, that every single member of it, man or woman, should be enabled to contribute his or her best to society. It is important to realise that society is relational: the foremost member of it can contribute the maximum he is capable of only if all other beneath him also contribute their full share. In a society where women's contribution is little, to that extent, man's contribution also is therefore, automatically vitiated.

If prosperous, healthiest and happiest conditions are to prevail in a society masculine and feminine must influence its work in harmony. Hence for any material and spiritual advancement of the nation, women's emancipation should be the first consideration.

A coherent policy for women has not only to provide for the rights of women; it should also ensure in explicit terms the genuine participation of them in all aspect of national life as being essential to the whole process of development policy. It is in the State's best interests to utilise the talents of all its members, regardless of sex, so that its each and every member stand to benefit. This is possible only if a national policy for action is evolved through wide discussion and debate keeping in view the following points:

(a) to minimise the conflict between national policies and laws, and policies and laws for women;

(b) to minimise the sex bias in the recruitment, working conditions, salaries, benefits and promotion right from the lowest level to the top jobs;

(c) to provide facilities for promotion and day care centres; educational and leisure services for children; day hospitals for workers for children; day hospitals for workers, dependents in need of treatment;

production of labour saving household devices at reasonable prices, and low cost housing complete with domestic services;

(d) to introduce new methods of job evaluation and an equitable status and position for male and female workers with regard to social security and fiscal arrangements;

(e) to launch careful exercise of surplus manpower and womanpower planning in all states;

(f) to create new jobs and some of these need to be identified as to be done by women only;

(g) to make provisions for reservation for women in all training institutions and professional colleges;

(h) to provide legal aid to the needy women at the state expenses; and

(i) to review the current policies regarding employment, training and education if the proposed objectives of mass education as enshrined in our Constitution are to become truely meaningful.

It would be desirable if our planning system be conformity with overall humanpower plans, and is expected:

— to keep to a closer watch on changes in occupational structure of the women labour force, without neglecting quantative considerations;

— to analyse in greater depth the new areas of their employment being opened up by the development process;

— to increase the women labour force's adaptability to changing employments requirements through the appropriate development of training and further education facilities;

— to develop new job openings and higher skill levels in the tertiary sector of the economy (particularly cultural and welfare services, sporting and social organisations), where educated women are in growing demand;

— to pay more attention to making full use of the skill potential of educated women.

Three stages can be identified in the above planning process:

(i) continuing to refine the methods employed, so as to achieve an even closer fit between supply and demand;

(ii) making greater use of the facilities for the training of graduate women so that, building on a foundation of sound general training, changed or additional humanpower demands can be met rapidly and effectively; and

(iii) further increasing the versatility and adaptibility of graduate women undergoing training, so that they may better measure up or adjust to unpredictable job requirements.

Obviously, the various anti-discriminatory measures mentioned earlier are exercise entirely by men sitting in governmental joint or tripartite bodies from which women are practically excluded. Deserving women must be associated with all committees carrying out new job evaluations, in administrative services responsible for placement, vocational guidance and training, on economic planning bodies drawing up employment creation policies and in the joint labour-management machinery for negotiating and concluding collective agreements machinery for negotiating and concluding collective agreements and last but not least to function as pressure groups to increase their participation in development strategies on women's issues.

No doubt, it is an acknowledged fact that women, by and large, are excluded from certain crucial economic, social and political activities, that their roles as wives and mothers are associated with fewer powers and prerogatives than are the roles of men with the result that there is a wide disparity in working force participation between the sexes.

The imperative need is to provide equality of status, roles and position to women keeping in view the constitutional directives. Improvement in the quality of the output of working is one way of enhancing their contribution to socio-economic development. The other and probably the more important aspect, is that of drawing into productive work women who are equipped to produce but do not.

Equally, and perhaps even more important, is the problem of non-usilisation of the protential of women in service sector and professions of different kinds. Women must engage themselves in productive work because "work out side home confers on them prestige and status as compared to housewife" (Gulati, 1975, p. 37). Let every adult man or woman whatever his or her social position, or accomplishments, may function as a citizen and as an individual in the task of nation building activities. It is necessary to harness the total human resources of community and to aim at an integrated development of the total humanpower.

There is need for the society to recognise the role of a woman and to appreciate that she has much to contribute to the family and to the community as man, if not more.

The imperative need is for systematic study and indepth research in the status, position and role of women from historical, sociological, cultural and economic perspectives. Hence, the real work still remains to be undertaken. Illiteracy, lack of training in basic skills, ineffective enforcement of labour laws and industrial awards, non-implementation of national policies, non-appraisal of job performances and not discarding traditional attitudes are the various cases of the vicious circle of underdevelopment and low productivity, poor conditions of health and welfare, which have most serious implication not only for women but for society as a whole and for future generation.

REFERENCES

Bernard, Jassie (1957). *Social Problems at Midcentury*, New York, Holt Reinchart and Winston.

Bhende, Asha A. (1975). "Demographic Changes and the Status of Women": *Journal of Family Welfare,* Vol. 22, No. 2, pp. 11-19.

Clark, Colin (1958). "The Economics of Housework", *Bulletin of the Oxford University Institute of Statistics,* Vol. 20, No. 2, pp. 205-11.

Dube, S.C. (1963), "Men's and Women's Rules in India", *Women in the New Asia,* Barbara E. Ward (Ed.), Unesco, Paris.

Gulati, Leela (1975). "Female Work Participation", *Economic and Political Weekly,* Vol. 10, Nos. 1-2, pp. 45-42.

Hate, C.A. (1969). *"Changing Status of Women"*. Allied Publishers. Bombay, pp. 192, 350.

Krauss, Wilma R. (1974). "Political Implications of Gender Roles: A

Review of the Literature", *The American Political Science Review,* Vol. 68, No. 4, pp. 1706-23.

Mazumdar, Veena (1976). "Workers in a Changing Economy", *Yojna,* Vol. 19, No. 7, pp. 15-19.

Wadhera, Kiron (1976). *"The New Bread Winners"*. Vshwa Yuwak Kendra, New Delhi.

9

Women Under Globalisation

> "Development that is imposed from the outside takes away from the people their power to guide their own destiny. People must feel that they can do things for themselves."
>
> ***—Professor Wangari Maathai, an interview with Development Forum (October 1986)***

Globalization, privatisation and liberalisation are the order of day. Every nation and every society is under its impact. Here we will try to assess the womenpower under the impact of globalization.

The challenge of the environment was become one of the "hottest society issues of the 90s". The key words of the 1980s in international development strategies were 'privatisation of enterprises and structural adjustment programmes' for developing countries. In the late fifties and early sixties when the international community began to examine development problems in the UN fora, *"Women's issues"*, remained submerged under the surface emerging much later on the agendas in 1970s as opposed to 1950s. They began to be recognised reluctantly as societal and cultural issues in 1980s.

Thus, there is a time lag of two decades between *women* and *development* agendas at the national and international levels. Current academic research and government policies seem to have established connections between *environment and development* or *women and development* more easily than *women and environment.*

It is notable that for purposes of education curricula, the important point is that, conceptually, women are usually linked to environmental problems through the processes of development. "Success stories" and "case studies" presented at the Global Assembly on Women and Environment at Miami in November 1991 demonstrated this connection in practical terms. These stories reflect that there is an organic connection between people's movements to halt the degradation of the planet and women's movements to change policies of governments to improve their condition of life. Ecology and economy are transformed when governments design policies to clear forests and contractors make room for factories.

Development, as traditionally understood, is about industrialisation, about building roads, about using women as cheap labour, about constructing schools and hospitals, about creating jobs and social inequalities, about settling vast populations and about displacing cultures. It is also about providing incomes above subsistence levels and it is about the steady movement of people from agriculture to industry, about eroding fields and forests and about constructing high-rise buildings and car parks. It is about losing land and getting jobs.

The key questions to be addressed are: how does one capture such global complexity? How should an educational curricula be designed in the world of today? What are the mechanisms by which communications for development would eliminate discrimination between women and men? How should the biases inherent in national structures based on race, class, geography, nationality and above all gender be avoided? This is a daunting task. The Ex-Secretary-General of the United Nations, Javier Perez de Cuellar conceptualised the connections between environment and development in this way:

> "The environment is where we live. It is the air we breathe, the water we drink, the soil that grown our food and gives us minerals: it is all living things that surround us. Development is what we do with these resources to improve our lives... We often damage our environment by having too much or too little. Overconsumption leads to waste which pollutes our environment and uses our resources... Crushing poverty and growing populations create great pressure on the environment...."

In what way does *overconsumption,* criminal waste of natural resources and perpetual poverty affect people? It must be stated at the outset that the majority of inhabitants of this earth, women and men, are seriously struggling to survive in poor enclaves of rich countries and informal economies of poor countries.

But there is a difference between how men survive and how women struggle! It is this *differential* which is the subject of this book and forms the basis of women's connection to sustainable development. Being very low in economic hierarchies, women are not usually responsible for the enormous waste of natural resources and yet they are more seriously affected by environmental degradation. Women do not participate in development strategies or policies and yet their livelihood depends heavily upon how these are conceived and formulated.

Women are not party to economic disasters and yet they are always called upon to cushion family life by providing minimum needs in crisis.

Despite these economic and social consequences, few policy statements made during the debate by the preparatory Committee for UNCED (August 91) connected women to the international economic or global environment at the macro-level.

The Committee focused on 'urbanisation of poverty', 'environmental expenditure', 'responsibility for waste' and "overconsumption" of natural resources of the North. From all these topics, women were omitted, being regarded as neither beneficiaries nor contributors.

Womenpower and Environment

Remarkably, there are some interesting historical precedents at the national and international levels of linking women with development and environment with development. One of the most delicate points before the Rio Conference was how to create a conceptual framework outlining boundaries between development and environment. Serious differences in approaches emerged between the North and the South, becoming ever wider on the eve of the Conference. Differences in approaches were mainly based on a pyramid of inherent inequalities among nations, within various "social groups" in a nation and among women and men within a family.

This traditional pyramidal structure has been inherited for over two centuries during which international economic and political relations were dominated by original metropolitan powers, who laid the foundations of the current rules of international law. Now, within international institutions, national structures and local communities, the globalisation process has begun: it will affect all citizens of the world, women more than men.

It is more and more difficult to distinguish matters of

national sovereignty or propriety and draw clearer lines between national and international issues. UNCED linked environment and development internationally, to facilitate national mechanisms to meet global challenges facing degradation of the planet. It is fascinating to note that there is a *sameness* about the difference between the North and South on the one hand and perception of women and men on the other. The key issues in both cases concern changing traditional relationships and creating a new basis of equality and partnership.

According to the South, this change should reflect firstly, adequate 'environmental space' to ensure the development of the South: and, secondly, it should modify global economic relationships to ensure its access to financial resources, the pool of technology, knowledge and world markets. These two strategic considerations according to the South Centre (see *Towards A Common Strategy of the South in the UNCED Negotiations and Beyond,* Geneva, 1991) would enable the South "to pursue a development process that is both environmentally sound and rapid enough to meet the needs and aspirations of its growing populations". As mentioned earlier, the preparatory Committee of UNCED linked the two topics in these words:"...that the gender dimension is important in implementing the Resolution on 'Women in Environment and Development' and that the Rio Conference should take due account of the Nairobi Forward Looking Strategies (NFLS), the relevant parts of which focus on women and development.

According to the UNCED Resolution, "... the national and inter-national emphasis on ecosystem management and the control of environmental degradation, should be strengthened and that women should be recognised as *active and equal participants in* this process..." (emphasis added). This resolution assumes that there has been progress an women since the adoption of the NFLS based on equal participation between women and men. It takes another step forward to contributing to changing relationships of women with the economy and society. Two pertinent questions emerge out of the 1991 UNCED Resolution mentioned above. First, what are the mechanisms by which women would be a part of the ecosystem management at the national and international levels? Second, through which mechanisms should women participate in the control of environmental degradation? Partial answers to these questions have already appeared at the 1991 *Global Assembly on Women and the Environment* mentioned above analysed in Part V.

At that Assembly, various recommendations were made by the NGOs and Regional Assemblies on increasing women's participation in decision-making and enhancing their status. The significant point of these recommendations is that there are various points of *convergence and commonalities* among women's groups and organisation across political structures, economic systems and cultural hierarchies.

The main points of convergence or consensus relate to the following themes:

(a) that the future Earth Charter, International Conventions and other relevant agreements should include men and women in all future rights and obligations;

(b) that the free flow of *environmentally friendly technology* be made available to men and women equally;

(c) that women should occupy a significant proportion of senior positions on panels, boards, parliamentary committees, ministries and public agencies as well as on delegations to the UN, including follow up of UNCED and any other organisation; and

(d) that needs and views of women must be incorporated in the establishment of national priorities in the management of human and natural resources.

The Global Assembly baseing itself on women's experiences at national levels arrived at some important conclusions, which brought together environmental concerns and development needs.

Priority Themes

- "Conservation of energy starts in the household and is often related to tasks women predominantly perform...";
- "Designers of all water supply and sanitation systems should be required to consult women who are the primary users in the home";
- "...Women have often found ways to deal with waste economically and safely, whether by recycling or by responsible consumer behaviour..."

Women and Development

On the position of women in the process of development, reference needs to be made to an international instrument which represents the views of the policy makers of 175 member Governments of the United Nations. The Nairobi Forward Looking Strategies (NFLS) adopted at the UN Decade for Women End Conference in June 1985 referred to earlier is a unique document in the history of international relations. It represents futuristic ideas based on a consensus of a large number of member States, the North and the South the East and the West—from different and sometimes opposing economic systems and variety of forms of government and political structures. This document contains a conceptual framework or a future vision for the advancement of women. The differing definitions of advancement of women in this document reflect the results of tough political negotiations that went on behind the scenes and in the corridors of the UN.

During its preparation deep divisions emerged particularly between the US and the Soviet Union, the North and the South in 1983 and 1984. The end result was that for the first time, the NFLS succeeded in designing and intergovernmental programme at the global level, by bringing women and development issues centrestage in international negotiations. The drafting and redrafting of concepts and notions by groups representing different governments during those two years shows once again the painful process of achieving global consensus through the procedures of the United Nations.

The main themes of the UN Decade for *Women, Equality, Development and Peace,* were refined and redefined at the international policy level in this document to enable the formulation of national policies, programmes and projects affecting women. In order to appreciate the views and aspirations of women on the above-mentioned themes, a simple summary of the conceptual framework might be attempted.

On participation of women in development generally, there are no concrete measures or recommendations beyond the stipulation that there should be "increased numbers in decision-making all levels". Under the equality theme, equal participation of women with men is envisaged within existing national institutions and structures by introducing specific policy measures. The theme, international peace and security in this document is connected to reducing defence budgets, various phases of disarmament and eliminating "all forms of violence". The violence originating from international conflict is given the same status as physical and institutional violence against women in communities and families. Subsequent research shows that there is a direct corelation in same forms of violence.

The glaring omission in the NFLS is the analysis of policy measures to promote women's rights as citizens. What are the political rights of women? Do women have the right to demand democracy within the family and their community? What is the meaning of democracy for women? Can these rights be linked in a cause and effect relationship to the national and international institutions which act as fixed and permanent barriers to enhancing women's status? To overcome these obstacles and go beyond the intergovernmental programme for women as set out in the NFLS, women's movements and women's organisations have subsequently formulated their own plans of action and agendas.

Through NGOs and other organisations, they have accorded another interpretation of paragraph III of the NFLS on enhancing women's status in society, which is openended. This paragraph refers to the sub-title, "special measures," which aim at *enhancing women's autonomy* in development.

What are the steps that women need to take to qualify for entry to "the mainstream of the development process" (as NFLS puts it)? It is precisely at the entry point of development that several doors appear to be closed to women. The above mentioned linkages at the international level help to define macro-concepts on which governmental or intergovernmental programmes and projects on women and development could be structured. At the ground level, however, procedures must be defined to ensure that women become promoters of a healthy environment and can control the deterioration of environmental conditions which adversely influence their daily lives, in small huts, in villages and shanty towns.

The vicious circle of women and poverty has become a fact of modern life. The majority of women are struggling to improve their immediate conditions by constantly reversing or modifying the adverse impact of governmental policies: demographic and economic, social and fiscal. What are the sources (governmental or non-governmental) from which their needs, aspirations and perspectives originate? How could these be linked in research, from local and national space to the regional and finally the international agendas.

What are the elements on which UNCED requested governments to prepare national reports on the role of women in Sustainable Development? Which Plan of Action will form the *information base* of government policies at UNCED?

Some examples from UN guidelines circulated to governments capture women's perspectives in detail, particularly at the micro-level and provide some references on which governments are requested to submit their reports:

— Basic information on the interaction between the development process and the environment;
— Identification of areas in which the national situation is affected by international conditions;

— Impact of poverty, external debt and other economic factors on the protection of the global environment: and

— Goals and targets on pollution control, reduction in greenhouse gas emissions, toxic chemicals and hazardous substance management.

Work and Womenpower

It is pertinent to note that within a wider focus on the globalisation of the economy and its impact on lower income groups in developed and developing countries, the international policy package is tied together with women's work at the base. The remunerated and the unremunerated work of women are the mainstay of development concept having a direct impact on natural resources. During the last three decades, a series of questions on women's work has emerged on the social horizon, placing another obstacle in the uneven path of women's relationship to society.

The imbalance curve of their work and economic rewards trace hidden inequalities at various levels: among countries, within groups and inside families. At the same time, the combination of new social awareness and hard realities particularly the results of the economic policies of the 1990s have outlined the contours of a new phenomenon. Two elements of this are conspicuous at the level of analysis. First, the present position of women is related to the steady increase in the participation rates of women in the labour force in industrialised countries since the 1950s. The second element concerns the nature of women's work in most rural and urban areas of developing countries which is neither rewarded nor officially recognised. Both of these elements are interrelated and form two pieces of a larger puzzle. In the world economy; the cause and effects of these phenomena has not yet been clearly analysed nor linked to the globalisation processes in research.

An example of this lack of analysis would be the impact of the new "free trade" regime as envisioned in the Uruguay Round of Negotiation under the auspices of General Agreement of Tariffs and Trade (GATT). As an Indian environmental activist, Vandana Shiva, puts it, "...Liberalisation of trade will devastate women farmers and wage earners and further diminish their control over natural resources."

No doubt, there is enough evidence to show that the modalities of existing relationships of women to society have been questioned at various times and at various levels in recent history. But these challenges have never been so consistently and systematically presented as during the UN Decade End Conference in Nairobi in July 1985 discussed above. The accomplishments of the UN Decade for Women, its history of negotiations, its assessment of different regions and its final international consensus in the Nairobi Forward-Looking Strategies (NFLS) have been referred to earlier. Some questions still remain: What were the core issues then and now? First, are women left outside the decision-making processes of major economic and social concerns of this century? What are the economic causes which contribute to the pyramid of global inequalities, from the household to the national and international levels? In what way is the development process itself clogged to support women playing a secondary role?

To these prime questions still on the international agenda in 1991, the United Nations Environmental Programme (UNEP) contributing to UNCED added another dimension: that of sustainability to women's issues.

According to the Preamble of the *Resolution on Women and the Environment*. "... Development must not only increase standards of living, but must also improve the quality of life of men and women equally ...development must not destroy the ecological base on which critical life support systems, such as water, soil, and forests on which human survival is dependent."

The 'quality of life' is a term often used in UN decisions and resolutions. But its hidden and behind the scenes *raison d'etre* is omitted. Simply put, women contribute two-thirds of work hours to the world economy without being remunerated. The relationship of unpaid to paid work of women explains in part the hidden processes of globalisation of the world economy.

Women support a large part of the world economy by 'free services' in the home and the community. Women have always been *at work,* only the definitions of "work" and "workplace" in history have not been realistic enough to include their contribution to the economy and society. In the period of dynamic economic and social change during the last two centuries, questions relating to the size, nature and value of women's work were often left to sociological speculation emanating in myths and legends which have detailed systematic inquiry.

The result of wearing social blinkers for such a long time by mainstream researchers has been that the existing historical data and empirical evidence tend to lean heavily towards one side, particularly on "traditional roles". This has led to the analysis of women's status and workload in the subsistence economies of the Third World or testing the validity of the hypothesis of the "dual concept" of women in public and private spheres or linking different cultural values to behavioural patterns of societies.

From the steady gathering of accumulated data from 1970-1990, some primary conclusions are now beginning to emerge. There is a basic link between the large-scale economic structural change and social perspectives on women's work and cultural value systems. One of the main research conclusions is that the majority of the existing "industrial models" applicable in the North and the South are detrimental to the condition of women and have an adverse impact on their work and welfare.

The 1990 Commonwealth Report of the Ministers Responsible for Women's Affairs has suggested that while male workers can relate easily to wage labour, transition from a rural to an industrial economy destroys women's traditional place and opportunity to earn income in the production process. Furthermore, it damages their capacity to exercise a certain degree of control over their conditions of work and environment.

Another significant research insight that confirms this conclusion is the analysis of recent world surveys and reports: the very fact that women became an integral part of the "assembly line" in urban economies shows that when women have income of their own, they are released from the oppressive feudal structures left behind in rural areas. Thus industrialisation processes become a double-edged sword for women. The shifting of the earlier neat division of labour between men and women within the farm and the household could be directly connected to the vagaries of the international economy. The basic commodities, cocoa, tea, sugar, coffee nuts, bananas, rubber, fruit and flowers and clothing are exported regularly from the South to the North. Some of these commodities or primary products are grown, harvested and processed by women in developing countries; who continue to work with outdated tools and techniques. Others work with sewing machines, typewriters, and electronic spare parts to make a bare living. The reality for women is: Simple definition of development which translates into a "strategy of survival".

The shift from the agricultural sector to an urban milieu always affects the nature of women's work, their capacity to perform, their productivity levels, their position in the family and finally, their status in society. Irrespective of the political form of government, or the economic and social system or the model of industrialisation, what appears to be almost universally valid is that women's work is not yet fully recognised as "work" in the comprehensive sense of the term. Most of it is neither *socially valued* nor *economically rewarded* and this, despite the obvious fact that in almost all societies women are permanently working with a range of skills which are crucial for the economic and social well-being of most countries.

In fact, the paradox appears to be that the most socially significant occupations of food security, health care, education programmes and other social services that support any economic system are the responsibility of women. It is evident that because women work in these *feminine areas,* their occupations are regarded as low status, are frequently low paid and, in the hierarchy of economies, almost always considered low-skilled. Low status, low pay and low skills are the three pillars on which the work performance of women have rested for a long time. The sum total of this could be described as "non-status of women's work". This permanent and perpetual 'non-status', in turn, affects women's lives in a myriad of ways: they are tied down to family responsibilities, unable to move out of their grooves despite the fact that a large percentage of economically active women' support the world 'economy and cushion the social system in time of crisis. Recent data compiled by the UN has indicated that in several countries the official statistics continue to underestimate women's work. The new statistical techniques of qualification are not being applied to women's 'non-economic' activities.

There has been also serious controversy on what constitutes 'economic activity'. For reasons of bias and prejudice is systems of quantification much of what women do or perform has been officially defined as 'non-economic activity'. Of recent, there is a slight change in earlier definitions and a slow movement towards correcting underestimation and undervaluation of women's work by the application of new statistical concepts and economic definitions.

One main area of darkness, however, remains for the ensemble of "human rights" in Covenants, Treaties and Constitutions. Do women have the *right* to work? The legal answers seem to vary in different countries and have differential impact on women's income. There are several references to the right to work in UN Covenants and several ILO Standards, which implicitly or explicity recognise women's right to work. For example, in the operative part of the *Universal Declaration of Human Rights,* 1948, it is stated that "everyone has the right to work, to free choice of employment." Everyone here, is deemed to include both men and women.

There are other International Standards, which explicitly emobody the principle of non-discrimination on the grounds of sex, for example, Article 2 of ILO Convention on Discrimination on Employment and Occupation, No. 111 of 1958. Considering the uncertainties of interpretation, there was an explicit recognition of women's right to work at the 60th session of the International Labour Conference in 1975.

The conference adopted a Declaration and two Resolutions on Equality of Opportunity and Equality of Treatment for Women Workers in the International Women's Year. The most recent exponent of this principle is the UN Convention on the Elimination of All Forms of Discrimination Against Women (CEDAW), adopted in 1979 which came into force in 1981, and is now ratified by over 120 countries. The spirit of the new and emerging international economic and social norms has been reflected in national legislation of some countries. For example, the Constitutions of some states—Algeria, Bangladesh, Cuba, Hungary, Mexico, Portugal, Spain and the former USSR—directly refer to women's right to work. Interestingly, most Commonwealth countries are not included in this list. Several other countries, for example, the Federal Republic of Germany, Italy, Switzerland, India, Jamaica and Canada, while not directly mentioning women's right to work, have incorporated legal guarantees in national legislation, for example, on equal opportunity in employment between men and women.

The twelve European Economic Community countries, on the other hand, provide direct recourse to the courts in case of violation of the right to exercise an occupation, among others. But, there is a diversity of situations in many countries and at several levels. But, there is an increasing recognition of this right at formal policy levels by several governments, who have not adopted laws or made formal policy statements on this matter. By adopting laws to prohibit employers from discriminating between women and men in conditions of employment.

REFERENCES

1. Dr. EVa Rathgaber, "Integrating Gender Into Development: Research and Action Agenda for the 1990s," IDRC working paper, 1990.
2. See *"Success Stories," Global Assembly, Op. cit.*
3. See *"The International Policy Package,* Part II.
4. ILO, *Women at Work,* Special issues on Employment for Women (1975-1985): an ILO contribution to the UN Decade for Women, 1/1984.
5. Vandana Shiva, "Sustainability and viability of global market prescriptions" *Our Indivisible Environment,* FAO-FFHC/AD Workshop Report on South Asian Environmental Perspectives, Bangalore, October 1-7, 1990.
6. *Final Report,* Global Assembly of Women and the Environment, "Partners in Life", Maimi, 4-8 November 1991.
7. ILO Editorial, *Women at Work,* Geneva, 1/1978.
8. Commonwealth Secretariat, *Report, Third Meeting of Commonwealth Ministers Responsible for Women's Affairs,* Ottawa, Canada, 9-12 October 1990.
9. Swasti Mitter, *Common Fate, Common Bond,* London, 1988.

Bibliography

Anderson, R.B.W. (1967). "On the Comparability of Meaningful Stimuli in Cross-Cultural Research." *Sociometry,* 30:124-126.

Bernard, Jassie (1957). *Social Problems at Midcentury,* New York, Holt Reinchart and Winston.

Bhende, Asha A. (1975). "Demographic Changes and the Status of Women": *Journal of Family Welfare,* Vol. 22, No. 2, pp. 11-19.

Chekki, D.A. (1974). *Modernisation and Kin Network.* London: E.J. Brill.

Chekki, D.A. (1978). *The Sociology of Contemporary India.* Columbia, Missouri: South Asia Books.

Clark, Colin (1958). "The Economics of Housework", *Bulletin of the Oxford University Institute of Statistics,* Vol. 20, No. 2, pp. 205-11.

Commonwealth Secretariat, *Report, Third Meeting of Commonwealth Ministers Responsible for Women's Affairs,* Ottawa, Canada, 9-12 October 1990.

Cromwell, R. and Olson, D. Editors (1975). *Power in Families.* New York: Halstead Press.

Dube, L. (1974). "Sociology of Kinship." Pp. 233-366 in *A Survey of Research in Sociology and Social Anthropology.* Bombay: Popular Prakashan.

Dube, S.C. (1963), "Men's and Women's Rules in India",

Women in the New Asia, Barbara E. Ward (Ed.), Unesco, Paris.

Duijkar, C.S. (1935). *Comparative Research in Social Science.* International Social Science Bulletin No. 7.

EVa Rathgaber, "Integrating Gender Into Development: Research and Action Agenda for the 1990s," IDRC working paper, 1990.

Ghadially, Rehana (Ed) *Women in Indian Society*, New Delhi. Sage Publication, 1988.

Gore, M.S. (1968). Urbanisation and Family Change. Popular Prakashan.

Gulati, Leela (1975). "Female Work Participation", *Economic and Political Weekly,* Vol. 10, Nos. 1-2, pp. 45-42.

Hartley, R. (1962). "Children's Perceptions and Expressions of Sex Preference" *Child Development* 33: 221-227.

Hate, C.A. (1969). *"Changing Status of Women"*. Allied Publishers. Bombay, pp. 192, 350.

Heer, D.M. (1963). "The Measurement and Bases of Family Power, an Overview." *Marriage and Family Living,* 25: 133-39.

Hughes, Mary and Kennedy, Mary, *New Futures: Changing Women's Education*, Routledge and Kegan Paul, 1985.

ILO Editorial, *Women at Work,* Geneva, 1/1978.

ILO, *Women at Work,* Special issues on Employment for Women (1975-1985): an ILO contribution to the UN Decade for Women, 1/1984.

Indra Sawhney vs. *Union of India,* AIR 1993 SC 477: (923 SUP- SCC 217).

Kali's Yug-Women and Law Journal, March 2000, p. 62.

Kardiner, A. and Linton, R. (1939). *Individual and His Society,* New York: Columbia University Press.

Khatri, A.A. (1962). "Social Change in the Hindu Caste Family and its Possible Impact on Personality and Mental Health." *Sociological Bulletin,* 11: 1-2, 1962. (Presented at Indian Sociological Society Meeting, Mysore, 1962).

Khatri, A.A. (1966). "Marriage and Family in India: An Overview of Researches." Part II of *Researches in Child Development, Marriage and Family Relations Done in Indian Institutions of Teaching and Research,* University of Baroda, Baroda, (Presented at Interdisciplinary Seminar, University of Baroda, 1965).

Khatri, A.A. (1970). "Personality and Mental Health of Indians (Hindus) in the Context of their Changing Family Organisation." A Chapter in *Child in His Family,* edited by James Anthony and Cyrille Koupernik. New York: John Wiley and Sons.

Khatri, A.A. (1971). *A Scale to Measure Jointness of Families in India,* Ahmedabad: B.M. Institute.

Khatri, A.A. (1974a). "Heterosexual Friendship and Involvement in Mate Selection Process of Primary and Secondary Teacher Trainees in Ahmedabad." A chapter in the Family in India: A Regional view, edited by George Kurian, Mouton The Hague.

Khatri, A.A. (1974b). "Parental Preference for a Boy or a Girl and Their Rationale as Perceived by East Indian Children." Presented at the Committee in Family Research, VIII World Congress of Sociology held during August, 1974 at Toronto, Canada.

Khatri, A.A. (1975a). "The Adaptive Extended Family in India Today, "Journal of Marriage and the Family, 35:3, 1975. (a Modified version of the paper presented at American Sociological annual meeting at Montreal, Canada, 1974).

Khatri, A.A. (1975b). "Decision-making and Mutual Consultation Among Hindu Families in India." Presented at Southern Sociological Society Meeting, Washington, D.c., April, 1975.

Khatri, A.A. (1979). "Power in Families of American and East Indian Colleges Students, "Presented at the Annual Meeting of the Southern Sociological Society, April, 1979 at Atlanta.

Khatri, A.A. (1983). *Marriage and Family Relations Through Literature*. Mandvi-Kutch: Scintilla Publications. Distributors: New York: General Hall.

Khatri, A.A. (1985). "Some Dimensions of Asiatic Indian Family: A Quantitative." A paper presented at the annual Meeting of the American Sociological Association Meeting at Washington, D.C. during August, 1985.

Khatri, A.A. and Siddiqui B. (1969). "A boy or a Girl? Preference of Parents for Sex of the Offspring as Perceived by East Indian and American Children: A Cross-Cultural Study." *Journal of marriage and the Family,* 31:2, 388-392.

Krauss, Wilma R. (1974). "Political Implications of Gender Roles: A Review of the Literature", *The American Political Science Review,* Vol. 68, No. 4, pp. 1706-23.

Kuppuswami, B. (1962). Manual of Socio-Economic Status Scale (Urban). Delhi: Mansayan.

Madhu Kishwar, "Taking on the Challenge", *The Hindustan Times,* May 16, 1996.

Madhu Kishwar, "Women and Politics: Beyond Quotas", *Economic and Political Weekly,* October 26, 1996, p. 2867.

Mazumdar, Veena (1976). "Workers in a Changing Economy", *Yojna,* Vol. 19, No. 7, pp. 15-19.

Minneapolis: National Council of Family Relations.

National Perspective Plan for Women (1988-200 A.D.) Report of the Core Group set up by the Department of Women and Child Development, Ministry of Human Resources Development, Government of India, 1988.

Peterson, K.K. (1969). "Kin Network Research: A Plea for Comparability." *Journal of Marriage and the Family,* 31: 275-280.

Pillai, J.K. *Readings in Women's Education*, Kodaikanal, Mother Teresa Women's University, 1988.

Pramila Dandvate, "...like a flower pot in a drawing room", *The Times of India,* July 21, 1996.

Ravinder K. Verma and Gyanender K. Verma, "Women in Bihar Politics", *Economic and Political Weekly,* April 13, 1996, p. 935.

Safilio-Rothschild, C. (1970): "The Study of Family Power Structure" in C.R. Broderic (ed.) *"A Decade of Family Research and Action.*

Scanzoni, J. and M. Szinovacz, (1980). *Family Decision-making,* Beverly Hills: Sage Publications.

Scazoni, J. (1979). "Social Processes and Power in Families". In Westley Burr et al., (Eds.) *Contemporary Theories about the Family.* New York: Free Press.

Shah, A.M. (1974). *The Household Dimension of The Family in India.* Berkeley: University of California.

Shanta Serbjeet Singh, "A Feminine Critique", 1998, p. 22.

Slipman, Sue. *Helping Ourselves to Power*, Oxford. Pergamon Press, 1986.

Sushieela Kaushik, "Why Women in Legislatures", Paper presented at the Meet of Parliamentarians (NCW), November 19, 1996.

Swasti Mitter, *Common Fate, Common Bond,* London, 1988.

Towards Equality: Report of the Committee on the Status of Women in India, Government of India, Department of Social Welfare, Ministry of Education and Social Welfare, New Delhi, December 1974.

Usha Narayanan, "Women's Political Empowerment: Imperatives and Challenges", *Mainstream,* April 10, 1999, p. 1.

Vandana Shiva, "Sustainability and viability of global market prescriptions" *Our Indivisible Environment,* FAO-FFHC/AD Workshop Report on South Asian Environmental Perspectives, Bangalore, October 1-7, 1990.

Wadhera, Kiron (1976). "*The New Bread Winners*". Vshwa Yuwak Kendra, New Delhi.

Index